The Geopolitics
of the
Nuclear Era:
*Heartland, Rimlands,
and the Technological
Revolution*

COLIN S. GRAY

The Geopolitics of the Nuclear Era:

Heartland, Rimlands, and the Technological Revolution

COLIN S. GRAY

PUBLISHED BY

Crane, Russak &
Company, Inc.
NEW YORK

National Strategy
Information Center, Inc.

**The Geopolitics of
the Nuclear Era**
Published in the United States by
Crane, Russak & Company, Inc.
347 Madison Avenue
New York, N.Y. 10017

Copyright © 1977 National Strategy Information Center, Inc.
111 East 58th Street
New York, N.Y. 10022

Library Edition: ISBN 0-8448-1257-9
Paperbound Edition: ISBN 0-8448-1258-7
LC 77-83666

Strategy Paper No. 30

Printed in the United States of America

Table of Contents

Preface

Why should an editor, labor leader, businessman, or Member of Congress address himself to so arcane and forbidding a subject as "geopolitics"? To many ears, the term connotes the jingoism of a bygone era. Modern man, animated by concerns about racism and human rights, finds it distasteful to contemplate raw politics, seapower, and economic warfare. (How much more pleasant to pacify the jungle of national sovereignties with cultural exchanges and protest marches against breeder reactors.)

But even a mild Social Democrat like Helmut Schmidt has warned that we face, in the coming decade, a "struggle for the world product." Already, ignorant gunboats may clash by night over access to fish protein and offshore oil. The age of detente is shading into the era of the resource war, as Soviet policy presumably seeks to seal off mineral-rich Africa from the United States, Japan, and the EEC. And the Strait of Hormuz may involve us in a war sooner—and for more valid reason—than the Panama Canal; for, in this case, geography is energy, energy is economics, economics is security, and security is "geopolitics."

In *The Geopolitics of the Nuclear Era*, Colin S. Gray explores the often overlooked relation of geographical setting and physical power to international politics. Through geopolitical analysis, he argues, it is possible to understand trends and historical continuities, and approach the security problems of the West within a global framework. In this context, he examines the roots and dynamic functioning of Soviet conflict strategy, and stresses the global policy implications for the United States and its allies of the Soviet military build-up of the 1970s.

The current shift of relative power and influence to the Soviet Union is especially alarming when viewed in geopolitical perspective. Drawing from concepts contained in the classic literature of geopolitics, Gray concentrates on the inherent struggle between the "Heartland" power of the Soviet Union and the maritime alliance led by the United States for effective defense of the "Rimlands" of Eurasia-Africa and their adjacent seas. The author reminds us of the geopolitical imperative that the Heartland and Rimlands must never be dominated by a single political will. Gray views the current Soviet build-up of military and naval capability as an historic bid by the Soviet Union for hegemony over these Eurasian-African Rimlands, and thus—by extension—for leverage against the rest of the world.

The United States and its allies have the human and material resources to resist the Soviet bid for world hegemony; but neglect of geopolitical analysis may cause the United States to underestimate the magnitude of the current Soviet threat. Denial of Soviet domination of the Eurasian-African Rimlands and maintenance of relatively free access to the "Rimland resources" and their adjacent seas are vital security interests of the United States. By examining current trends in international politics within a geopolitical context, Gray seeks to outline an appropriate framework of assumptions for the analysis of East-West relations which will contribute to Western foreign policy needs.

The author, who is now on the Professional Staff of the Hudson Institute, was educated at Manchester and Oxford Universities, and holds a D.Phil. from the latter institution. He has taught at the Universities of Lancaster and British Columbia, and served on the staffs of the Canadian Institute of International Affairs and the International Institute for Strategic Studies. He is the author, among other works, of _The Soviet-American Arms Race_ (1976) and _Strategic Studies and Public Policy_ (forthcoming).

Frank R. Barnett, _President_
National Strategy Information Center, Inc.

September 1977

Author's Note

No short text on geopolitics can possibly do justice to the richness and scope of its subject matter. This study has two biases which need to be recognized explicitly at the outset. I am a professional defense analyst, and my background and orientation is European-Atlantic rather than Asian-Pacific. Hence, some readers may find that the argument bears down too heavily upon military issues and is overly concerned with European questions. By way of self-defense, I can only offer the consideration that I see this study as a contribution to what I hope will be a long-overdue revival of explicitly geopolitical analysis. Nothing would please me more than for Asian-oriented political scientists/strategists, or for international economists, to be spurred by this study to engage in geopolitical analysis that reflected their areas of professional training and concern.

Geopolitics as a policy science has the merit of requiring analysts and commentators to stand back from the detail of contemporary debate and ask, "What does it mean?" Geopolitical perspectives enable the specialist and the layman to understand trends and historical continuities that may not even be comprehended by the initiators of the policy actions under study. In practice, geopolitical lore permeates our thought (and action) on international relations, but it tends to be unacknowledged and to lack discipline. I hope that this study will encourage some readers to examine (or re-examine) their culturally-bequeathed mental world-maps, and consider the *global* policy implications for the United States and its allies and friends of the Soviet military build-up of the 1970s.

Colin S. Gray

1

Geography and Policy

The United States must recognize once again, and permanently, that the power constellation in Europe and Asia is of everlasting concern to her, both in time of war and in time of peace.[1]

We shall continue to depend primarily on our own national strength, for we know that the failure of a great state to consider power means its eventual destruction and conquest. It has meant the downfall of all the empires that have been tempted by the flabby ease of unpreparedness.[2]

States are always engaged in curbing the force of some other state. The truth of the matter is that states are interested only in a balance which is in their favor. Not an equilibrium, but a generous margin is their objective. There is no real security in being just as strong as a potential enemy; there is security only in being a little stronger. There is no possibility of action if one's strength is fully checked; there is a chance for a positive foreign policy only if there is a margin of force which can be freely used.[3]

In a world of international anarchy, foreign policy must aim above all at the improvement or at least the preservation of the relative power position of the state. Power is in the last instance the ability to wage successful war, and in geography lie the clues to the problems of military and political strategy. The territory of a state is the base from which it operates in time of war and the strategic position which it occupies during the temporary armistice called peace. Geography is the most fundamental factor in the foreign policy of states because it is the most permanent.[4]

---

[1] Nicholas J. Spykman, *The Geography of the Peace* (New York: Harcourt, Brace, 1944), p. 60.
[2] *Ibid.*, p. 60.
[3] Nicholas J. Spykman, *America's Strategy in World Politics, The United States and the Balance of Power* (Hamden, Conn.: Archon, 1970; first published 1942), p. 21.
[4] *Ibid.*, p. 41.

1

The Argument

Sound foreign policy, and the design of its effecting instruments (diplomatic, military, economic, subversive, and cultural), can flow only from a secure grasp of appropriate premises for thought, declaration, and action. It is the contention of this author both that such premises may be discovered through disciplined, openminded inquiry, and that Western policy in general, and American policy in particular, have succumbed of recent years to numerous fashionable shibboleths that do not speak to the vital interests of Western societies. This study has a constructive rather than a destructive purpose. The primary intention is to outline an appropriate framework of assumptions for the analysis of East-West relations. It is necessary first, however, to register the fact that this inquiry had its genesis in an appreciation of the inadequacy of contemporary American foreign policy, and the folly in the pseudo-sophistication of much of what passes for instruction in international relations in many universities.

The author of the quotations which preface this chapter, Nicholas Spykman, has appeared on very few university book lists in the 1970s. This is unfortunate, because—for all the admittedly dated details—Spykman directs the student toward the important and the enduring, as opposed to the trivial and the transient. Many "approaches" to the study of international relations are indeed possible and defensible, but there is really only one "approach" which enables students to appreciate the essence of the field. The approach, for want of better terminology, is *power politics*. Too many introductory courses in international relations treat power politics as a passing phase in the history of academic international relations scholarship. Students are told that power politics emerged in the late 1930s, heralded unambiguously by the publication of E.H. Carr's *The Twenty Years' Crisis* in 1939,[5] and matured with the appearance of the first edition of Hans Morgenthau's *Politics Among Nations* in 1948.[6] Through the 1950s, so the story goes, power politics was the dominant scholarly and policy-relevant paradigm, with strategic studies presenting a special case of that approach—"power politics with nuclear weapons."[7] Since the late 1950s, to proceed, international relations as a nascent discipline has moved to higher plateaux of sophistication and methodological rigor.

Unfortunately, through the malign synergistic effect of a misplaced quest for scientific knowledge and a quite premature "professionalization,"

---

[5] (London: Macmillan, 1939).
[6] (New York: Knopf, 1948).
[7] I am indebted for this phrase to Professor James King of the Naval War College, Newport, Rhode Island.

the student of international relations has, over the past two decades, increasingly been protected from an understanding of the essential character both of international relations in the large, and of contemporary international relations as they effect him or her. Evidence of the Iron Law of Triviality may be gleaned impressionistically from attendance at professional gatherings of international relations scholars or, more rigorously, from a survey of the contents of the pertinent professional journals.[8]

There are, of course, many possible frameworks for the attempted understanding of international relations; most probably have *some* value, but—most emphatically—all are not of equal worth for the comprehension of the more important features of world political processes. In very large measure, the academic study of international relations has "taken off" into self-sustained growth in a direction very largely irrelevant to what one must call the real world. This study focuses upon the most pressing, dangerous, and potentially fatal fact of the real world—namely, that we are at the mid-stage of a shift in relative power and influence to the Soviet Union that is of historic proportions, and which promises, unless arrested severely, to have enduring significance. This easily-demonstrated fact does not detract from the importance of other processes, sometimes only distantly related, that are eroding familiar structures in international relations. There has been a shift in global economic/financial power, acquiesced in by Western governments, toward major oil producers; and the force of national feeling has greatly complicated the calculations of those who are (or were) wont to see local "actors" as pawns in a global superpower chess game. But the rise in Soviet standing in the world, which may be traced almost exclusively to the increase in relative Soviet military capabilities, both dwarfs other concerns in its immediacy and seriousness, and renders other problems far less tractable.

The first duty of a government is to ensure, to the extent feasible, the physical security of its citizens—a duty closely followed by the requirement that the core values, other than physical survival, of the society should be protected and, if possible, advanced. The principal threat to the survival of American citizens, and to the endurance of their values, lies in the ambitions that energize Soviet military power. It is easy to be misunderstood. The author does not claim, in this study, to be addressing the totality of international relations; he does not deny that there are several distinct, if linked, functional "chessboards" that are properly the concern of scholars

---

[8] *International Studies Quarterly* and *Journal of Conflict Resolution* are the principal scholarly monuments to irrelevance.

of international relations.[9] What he does claim, without qualification or apology, is that the military-diplomatic "chessboard" is, objectively, the most important, and that far too few scholars are addressing it. Alas, fashionable shibboleths attract many of the better brains even among those few who do choose to study military-diplomatic problems. Where once arms control was seen as a special subject subordinate, or at least complementary, to the consideration of strategy, today arms control questions are approached by many as though they were of primary significance, superordinate to strategic issues. But the main problem for the United States and NATO-Europe is not to secure tolerable SALT and MBFR agreements, prominent though those are in terms of the diplomatic agenda. Rather it is the problem of the design *and implementation* of a defense program that speaks realistically to foreign policy needs. Such a defense program will provide all of the "bargaining chips" that are necessary for effective arms control negotiation.

To summarize. The academic practitioners of international relations analysis and theory appear, very substantially, to have forgotten that their subject matter, stripped of secondary concerns, is about physical survival and relative influence. In short, to have recourse to the unfashionable but essential concept, it is about *power*. Power, moreover, does not bear solely upon security in its principal negative aspect (freedom from fear of attack); it also is relevant to the advancement of a society's values. The political, economic, and social liberties valued by Americans do depend, to a significant degree, upon American capability and willingness to project power. Many erudite analyses have demonstrated the ambiguity of power as a central organizing concept. But if the concepts of power, the balance of power, and national interest are interred (overtly, at least) for reason of lack of precision in meaning, upon what basis does one order one's thoughts concerning international political processes? Because scholars apparently have extreme difficulty coping with the multidimensional concept of power, it should not follow that—as supposedly responsible educators of the young and uniquely qualified, specialized contributors to the public weal—they are, therefore, at liberty to pursue their inquiries along empirically more manageable tracks. The neglect of relative power questions may, quite literally, kill us.

Freed from the discipline of attention to, or appreciation of, relative power issues, the professor of international relations and his unfortunate students are rudderless in a highly dangerous world. Students, who are the

---

[9] See Stanley Hoffman, "Weighing the Balance of Power," *Foreign Affairs*, vol. 50, no. 4 (July 1972), pp. 618-643.

next generation of officials, politicians, and media commentators, are introduced to the concepts of power, balance of power, and national interest in the same way that they are informed of the mysteries of systems, cybernetics, communications, transnational relations, and bureaucratic politics (and possibly even content analysis and simulation, if the professor truly cannot distinguish between approach and content). Thucydides and David Easton are granted equal standing.[10] Not infrequently, students sense the "trained incapacity" of their teachers to speak to the real world. But the well-established system of professionalization ensures that "proper" respect for the extant, fashionable wisdom of the discipline is induced.

This study has a limited focus and a limited purpose. It seeks to analyze the roots and the dynamic functioning of Soviet-American political rivalry. While many academic readers will doubtless be shocked by the fairly free use made here of the terms power and balance of power, they should be even more distressed by the *leitmotiv* of geopolitics. Orthodox and fashionable, or perhaps mainstream, analyses in the fields of international relations and strategic studies tend to make only the most minimal explicit use of geopolitical perspectives. But since mainstream analysis has either preached acquiescence over a progressive, adverse shift in the Soviet-American balance (or, more commonly, has chosen not to address the issue), has found much to be praised in the SALT exercise as conducted thus far, and is not disturbed unduly by the military-diplomatic implications of the deteriorating military balance in Europe and the modernization and forward deployment of Admiral Gorshkov's blue-water navy, the time is long overdue for a return to matters of fundamental significance. The prime virtue of geopolitics is that it does, when not abused (and any perspective may be granted an inappropriately grandiose mandate), direct attention to factors of enduring importance.

For the purposes of this study, geopolitics will be understood to refer to "the relation of international political power to the geographical setting."[11] Geography is a term that defies authoritative definition. As a (candidate) scholarly discipline, geography is what geographers do. Putting pedantry aside, this study is concerned to explore the relation of the physical environment, as perceived, molded, and utilized by men, to international politics. Therefore, attention is focused not solely upon the interacting perceptions of the spatial relationships between politically-organized seg-

[10] Thucydides, *The Peloponnesian War* (London: Penguin, 1954); David Easton, *The Political System* (New York: Knopf, 1959).
[11] Saul B. Cohen, *Geography and Politics in a Divided World* (London: Methuen, 1964), p. 24.

ments of topography, but also upon what for want of a better term should be called cultural geography.

The principal argument of this study is that the *leitmotiv* of the geopolitical perspective enables one to discern trends, and even patterns, in power relations. The meaning of physical geography is, of course, altered by technology and by national "moods" which emerge as specific, widespread responses to particular events. Nonetheless, while granting the very important qualification that power relations are inherently dynamic, it is still possible to claim that states do tend to pursue a reasonably steady course in their foreign policies. Moreover, not only do the instrumental goals of foreign policy tend to endure from administration to administration (or even from regime to regime), but so do the national "styles" with which those goals are pursued. The concept of national style is as critical to sound political and strategic analysis as it tends to escape explicit recognition. Despite occasional excess of ambition in the definition of policy goals, not to mention gross incompetence in policy implementation, it is important to recognize that states, over a long historical period, do tend to reach internal agreement over the "proper" scope, and instruments for the support, of their foreign policies. Similarly, states tend to repose confidence in individual ways, or styles, in foreign policy behavior.

The above argument, however important, is offered only as a limited, contingent guide to understanding. There is no substantial trace of determinism in this theme. Geopolitical factors—that is to say, both the operational environment (the world as it really is) and the psychological environment (the world as seen by conditioned and fallible human beings)— do not *require* that certain policies be adopted. Geopolitical relations open and foreclose upon ranges of policy possibilities—which societies and their governments may pursue or not as circumstance and mood take them.[12] While granting freedom of choice, the geopolitical perspective upon international politics does increase appreciation of those policies which are likely to be more, as opposed to less, successful—and those policies that will in all likelihood be more, as opposed to less, onerous to see through to successful conclusions.

The principal argument of this study, as stated above, is to encourage readers to think geopolitically about international relations. The principal motive underpinning this enterprise, however, is the fear on the part of the author that an historical bid for world hegemony on the part of the Soviet

---

[12] This theme is discussed at length in Harold and Margaret Sprout, *The Ecological Perspective on Human Affairs, With Special Reference to International Politics* (Princeton: Princeton University Press, 1965), particularly ch. 7.

Union is not appreciated for what it is by Western publics. The Soviet challenge and the pusillanimous character of the Western response both lend themselves to detailed explanation in geopolitical terms.

New Myths and Old Realities

Like Pavlov's dogs, human beings tend to respond by conditioned reflex. American and NATO-European societies appear to have been persuaded by their licensed opinion leaders that international relations may conveniently be periodicized. There was a period of "Cold War" that—according to taste—endured from 1945-47 until 1963-69, so the tale proceeds. A message central to this study, as it was to the works of the author whose thoughts preface this chapter (Nicholas Spykman), is that the struggle for power is a permanent feature of the partial anarchy that we term international relations. Argument all too easily slips into epithet and "code-word" charges. This text will undoubtedly attract the charge of "Cold Warriorism," despite the fact that the author rejects the concept of the Cold War. Some of the crasser anti-Soviet propaganda, and many of the more alarmist claims concerning Soviet military intentions, do indeed invite derision. Moreover, such literature is dysfunctional to Western interests since it serves to reinforce those fashionable prejudices that tend to promote a discounting of shrill cries to the effect that "the Russians are coming." Western publics properly versed in geopolitical lore, or at least broadly familiar with the arguments (if not the writings, directly) of Nicholas Spykman, and other socalled "realist" authors, would not need to be propagandized concerning, or even reminded of, international dangers.

The faltering detente processes of the mid-1970s are not intended by Soviet officials to promote the goal of a stable East-West power relationship. Soviet officials do not believe in stable power relationships—a stance that historically is beyond contention, yet which contradicts the aspirations of both conservative and, above all, liberal optimists in the West. This line of argument, unlike much in this study, does not lend itself to challenge. Soviet dedication to the idea of a permanency of struggle is both proclaimed openly for those who care to pay attention, and is easily deducible from Soviet behavior. Official Soviet endorsement of a conflict-dominated approach to international relations does not, thereby, condemn the world to particular political outcomes. Western devotion to the ambiguous concepts of stability and order can and should have major consequences for the character of international political life, provided Western societies never forget that every system of international order requires dedicated guardians. Stability and order do not occur as free goods, provided by some "hidden hand" bereft of muscular support.

As a commentary upon, rather than an addition to, the central argument of this study, it needs to be recognized that East-West conflict is (for all relevant policy-related purposes) a *permanent* feature of international relations. In the very long term, Soviet-American rivalry may wither away after the fashion of Christian-Muslim competition, But such a prospect can play no sensible part in the policymaking of the late 1970s.

Thus far, it should be observed, no distinction of note has been made between the Soviet Union as a unit of power and the Soviet Union as a functional church—the bearer of an ideology. The absence of precision is intentional. This author suspects very strongly that the domestic political character of Russia/USSR has a major impact upon Soviet foreign and defense policies. Since the question of ideology must be faced directly, however, it is appropriate to observe that the ideology that has nurtured every Soviet citizen whose *weltanschauung* was not already fully mature by November 1917, *obliges* its adherents to define non-Socialist (by Soviet definition) regimes as being, objectively, the enemies of the Soviet state. The term *enemies* is used very deliberately. Those Western officials and commentators who endorse some variant of an optimistic philosophy concerning the future character of East-West relations, would do well to study the Soviet Union both in terms of what the Soviet state tells its own people, and how official doctrine defines the nature of the foreign relations of the Soviet Union. Over the long term, Soviet officials know (courtesy of the ideology that constitutes the sole basis for the legitimacy of the political authority of the Communist Party of the Soviet Union—a point which often seems to escape notice in the West) that they are locked into a life-and-death struggle with antagonistic social systems.

Marxism-Leninism, even as amended for contemporary use/rationalization, is a global theory. Not merely do Soviet officials know, as a matter of elementary *realpolitik,* that interstate power relations are inherently dynamic; they also know that they have a historic mission to carry through the working out of the laws of historical development. This inalienable obligation to conflict does not prescribe war (although the concepts of war and peace are somewhat blurred in Soviet thinking)—or, indeed, any particular policy action at any particular time. But it does foreclose definitively upon any genuine endeavor to stabilize East-West relations, with proper regard being paid for the legitimate interests of non-Socialist states/societies. Indeed, the phrasing of the last sentence is an absurdity in Soviet terms. Just what the policy implications of this line of argument should be for Western countries may reasonably be disputed. What may not reasonably be disputed is the long-term and nonretractable nature of East-West conflict.

A comprehensive listing of widespread contemporary myths is not needed. What follows is the specification of those major myths which serve, at present, to detract from the level and character of support that vital Western interests require.

1. The Soviet Union may be bribed/persuaded into adopting a far less conflict-oriented framework for the conduct of its foreign relations.
2. Arms control processes speak to the *real* interests of both sides, and hence should provide a crucial means for defusing a major source of East-West tension.
3. Time is on our side. Soviet foreign and defense policies will be modified benignly (by Western interpretation) as the scientific-industrial revolution increases the bargaining power of technocratic elites/ interest groups/pressure groups, and as a simple consequence of the aging of the regime.
4. War between the Soviet Union and the United States cannot serve Soviet interests.

These four myths, or persuasive fallacies perhaps, are the product essentially of psychological projection. Humane and prudent Western beliefs are projected upon an alien political culture. As "old realities" rather than "new myths," the subjects of the four points cited above may be treated as follows:

1. Conflict between East and West is a permanent premise in Soviet thought—until the eventual demise of the political power of capitalism in the West. Periods of greater or lesser relaxation in the details and ambiance of Soviet foreign policy have, and can have, only a short-term tactical significance.[13]
2. Arms control, in the Soviet view, is but another process wherein the long-term political struggle is conducted. Armaments reflect political competition and will, and not *vice versa*. Military competition between the superpowers is dictated by the fundamental antagonisms between their societies. SALT, for example, has political symbolic value, but its consequences for Western security can be trivial at best and seriously

---

[13] See John Erickson, "Detente: Soviet Policy and Purpose," *Strategic Review*, vol. 4, no. 2 (Spring 1976), pp. 37-43.

disadvantageous at worst—save in the context of a major Western rearmament drive.

3. Time is not on our side. The Soviet Union is not evolving into a far more pluralistic and liberal society, wherein very serious domestic checks and balances would restrict the freedom of foreign policy action by the state. Western-oriented political science models just do not fit Soviet history or current reality. Although some minor qualifications could be offered, the most important facts to bear in mind concerning the nature of the Soviet polity are that it is a "command" system of a patrimonial state, that its leaders are fundamentally illiberal (by training, habit, and *for good reason*), and that the prospects for Soviet evolution into a distinctive, though recognizable, Western-style state are very close to zero.[14] Near total repression works. The present system of internal security, for all its vast wasteful aspects and the embarrassment that it occasionally generates in terms of foreign perceptions, provides for a domestic order, predictability, and stability that no Soviet leadership should be expected voluntarily to place at risk. The Soviet dissident "movement," for all its courage and conscience value, is reminiscent more of the aristocratic utopians of the 19th century than of a serious force for political change.

4. Whether or not war would serve Soviet interests will depend upon the evolution of the military balance, Soviet perceptions of Western political will, and the availability of appropriate nonmilitary policy options in crisis situations. In Soviet perspective, the more effective the Soviet ability to prosecute military action, the more likely should it be that Western governments will decline to offer military resistance to Soviet actions. Western societies have grown so used to the notion that "nuclear war is unthinkable," that extreme resistance is offered to the proposition that the threat of war could be employed for coercive, as opposed to dissuasive or deterrent, purposes. But the reality, as opposed to the Western-projected mythology, of the Soviet view of war is as follows. All weapons, including those of mass destruction, can serve political ends; victory is a meaningful, indeed essential, objective; and the levels of violence reached are determined by the political character of a war, not by the weapons that one *chooses* to employ; that is, Western theories of escalation and limited war are fundamentally

---

[14] A superb development of this line of argument is William E. Odom, "A Dissenting View on the Group Approach to Soviet Politics," *World Politics,* vol. 28, no. 4 (July 1976), pp. 542-567.

flawed, in the Soviet view, by their neglect of political factors.[15] In order to give effect to these ideas, the Soviet Union is engaged in a military modernization and augmentation program that touches upon all elements of military power.

Continuity and Change

It is suggested here that there is a way of looking at international relations that may properly, and without apology or excuse, be termed geopolitical. Furthermore, it is suggested that geopolitics is not simply one set of ideas among many competing sets that help to illuminate the structure of policy problems. Rather, it is a meta- or master framework that, without predetermining policy choice, suggests long-term factors and trends in the security objectives of particular territorially-organized security communities. Geopolitics flourished as a fashionable *explicit* framework for thought in the 1930s and early 1940s (in particular). Its decline in popularity may be traced to several major causes, prominent among which were the "guilt by association" with German *Geopolitik,* the natural working out of academic and popular-commentary fashion (which, by definition, has to change), and changes in military and civil technology.[16]

The *leitmotiv* for much geopolitical theorizing was, somewhat prematurely, the struggle between landpower and seapower. The coming of nuclear weapons, and particularly the means for their delivery over intercontinental distances without need for the support of forward bases, seemed to very many people to destroy the validity of the old, familiar geopolitical concepts. If super/great power strength *really* resided in centrally-based and centrally-targeted nuclear-capable weapon systems, and if the outcome of a major war would be decided in a matter of hours by means of the employment of the weapon systems on hand, the spatial concepts and relationships that structured geopolitical theory appeared to be almost completely irrelevant.

For reasons that this author has explained in detail elsewhere, it was not only geopolitical theory that was discarded, or simply neglected and then forgotten, as the nuclear era matured.[17] Prenuclear strategic *and* international political theory and experience (scarcely a small slice of human history), in general, tended to be ignored as scholars and officials grappled

[15] See Leon Gouré, Foy D. Kohler, and Mose L. Harvey, *The Role of Nuclear Forces in Current Soviet Strategy* (Washington: Center for Advanced International Studies, University of Miami, 1974).

[16] See ch. 2.

[17] In Colin S. Gray, "Across the Nuclear Divide: Strategic Studies, Past and Present," *International Security,* vol. 2, no. 1 (Summer 1977).

with the exciting and apparently novel problems posed by the galloping revolution in weapons/transportation technology.

In fact, the geographical landforms of Eurasia, and the insular character of the Americas *vis-à-vis* Eurasia, have posed—and continue to pose—problems for nuclear strategy that are still unresolved by responsible Western officials. The concepts contained in the classic literature of geopolitics were never so relevant to international political reality as they are today. Admittedly, the classic writings need some reinterpretation and must be approached with great caution, in view of the changed meaning that technology gives to geography. Nevertheless, the emphasis in this study is upon continuity rather than change. With few exceptions, the scholars and officials who have given direction to American thought and policy in the fields of foreign policy and strategy since the mid-1950s have been people heroically ill-versed in history and geography. Each problem has tended to be treated *sui generis*—or on its own merits, pragmatically, when the point is phrased positively.

Unfortunately, problems have a past and a future that rarely are immediately discernible on the basis of contemporary developments alone. Neither the disciplines (economics, mathematics, physics, law, political science [possibly]) nor the pseudo-disciplines (international relations, systems analysis/operations research) that have served as recruiting grounds for the majority of contemporary American foreign policy/strategic thinkers/actors, have produced people well-qualified to see beneath the surface of political and strategic events. The fields of inquiry that one might expect to educate people appropriately, political science and international relations, have to a very large extent divorced themselves from significant real-world concern in their dadaist pursuit of methodological purity. To make the complaint specific: a person who can design efficient nuclear weapons is, *ipso facto,* qualified neither to devise nuclear strategy nor to conduct SALT negotiations; while a person trained (rigorously!) in theories of international relations may have attained such a plateau of sophistication that he neglects to notice that real-life politicians and officials seek to accumulate *power* in pursuit of their definition of the *national interest*. This author does not in any way deprecate the training of receptive minds. His point rather is that such training, in the pertinent scholarly fields, could and should—to the general (and individual) advantage—be oriented more toward the significant and the empirical.

The nuclear age, socalled, has seen a depressing continuity with the prenuclear in state practice. Contrary to utopian/eschatological expectations, both the ends and the means of state policy have altered scarcely at all. The threshold of intolerable provocation for the unleashing of war has admittedly risen between nuclear-armed states and those closely allied to nuclear-armed states. Considered overall, however, the evidence of 1945-77 does not begin to justify the continuing scholarly neglect of prenuclear thought and practice that pervades the American foreign policy/defense community.[18]

---

[18] Correctives for this condition are beginning to appear. See Klaus Knorr, ed., *Historical Dimensions of National Security Problems* (Lawrence, Kansas: University Press of Kansas, 1976).

2

Geopolitics

Grand Theory

The history of geopolitical thought has been reasonably well presented elsewhere and hence will not be reproduced here.[19] In any event, this study seeks to advance the geopolitical analysis of current problems rather than to celebrate neglected classics. In order to emphasize the contemporary character of the concerns of this study, the basic geopolitical premises of the argument which follows in Chapters 3-4 will be stated, fairly baldly, before the scholarly roots of current concepts are presented.

East-West political relations may fruitfully be considered as a long-term and inalienable struggle between the insular *imperium* of the United States and the "Heartland" *imperium* of the Soviet Union. In terms of physical geography, Eurasia (with Africa) may be conceived of as a centrally-placed island (the "World-Island" of geopolitical literature), surrounded (loosely) by an "outer crescent" of islands (the Americas, Australia). The interface between the power of the Heartland and the maritime *imperium* of North America are the "Rimlands" of Eurasia-Africa and the marginal seas which lap the shores of those "Rimlands." As of the mid-1970s, in geopolitical terms, superpower conflict may be characterized as a struggle between a substantially landlocked Heartland superpower, and a substantially maritime-dependent (in security perspective) insular super-power for control/denial of control of the Eurasian-African "Rimlands."

The dangers of deterministic cartography have to be admitted. Because the earth is a globe, every point is surrounded by every other point. The

---

[19] See Cohen, *op. cit.*, ch. 2; Derwent Whittlesey, *German Strategy of World Conquest* (London: Robinson, 1942); Robert Strausz-Hupé, *Geopolitics, The Struggle for Space and Power* (New York: Arno, 1972, first published 1942); and Derwent Whittlesey, "Haushofer: The Geopoliticians," in Edward Mead Earle, ed., *Makers of Modern Strategy, Military Thought from Machiavelli to Hitler* (Princeton: Princeton University Press, 1941).

suggestive power of particular maps depends critically upon where those maps are centered. One can design maps to suggest almost any geopolitical hypothesis that one chooses. Differing coloration and the creative addition of arrows and other "pop art" symbols can transform politically relatively neutral maps into presentations of terrifying threats. Readers of weekly news magazines will be familiar with the technique. Map creation as propaganda has been ubiquitous in the 20th century and has been exposed admirably by Hans Speier and Nicholas Spykman.[20] But Speier and Spykman, alas, have vanished from student reading lists, while cartographic traps for the unwary still abound. The high point (or low point) in cartographic ingenuity was attained by German geopoliticians in the late 1930s and early 1940s.

In company with some geopoliticians of an earlier generation, this author would affirm the following beliefs.

1. Control of the World-Island of Eurasia-Africa by a single power would, over the long term, mean control of the world.
2. Land power and sea power meet/clash in the Eurasian-African Rimlands and marginal seas. Control of those Rimlands and marginal seas by an insular power is *not* synonymous with control of the World-Island, but it does mean the denial of eventual global hegemony to the Heartland power (that is, the Soviet Union).

The proximate "stake" in Soviet-American rivalry, today as ever since World War II, has been control over the future of Western Europe. To simplify, such control by the Soviet Union could be effected in three ways: (1) by military conquest; (2) by what has come to be termed, misleadingly, as "Finlandization"; and (3) by control of the principal energy source for Western Europe's scientific-industrial vitality—namely, Middle Eastern oil. Option two, "Finlandization," refers to a hypothetical situation wherein West European countries acquiesce in a *de facto* Soviet control over the more important features of their domestic and foreign policies. "Finlandization," aside from the special case offered in Soviet option three, would be accomplished via European perceptions of an in-theater military balance that was overwhelmingly favorable to the Soviet Union, and the precipitate decline in the credibility of extracontinental military intervention by the United States in aid of a potentially disastrous local military imbalance.

"Finlandization" probably is an irrelevant concept *vis-à-vis* Western

---

[20] Hans Speier, "Magic Geography," *Social Research*, September 1941, pp. 310-330; Spykman, *The Geography of the Peace*, ch. 2.

Europe as a whole, because Soviet behavior toward Finland is disciplined by the expectation of adverse reactions in the policies of neutral Sweden, neutralist Yugoslavia, and NATO-Europe. If Western Europe were no longer locked into a security system with the United States, and its governments were prepared to be "friendly" toward expressed Soviet interests, what would prevent the Soviet Union from exercising virtually any kind of control that it found expedient? In practice, the strongest argument likely to discourage the Soviet exercise of Polandization or GDR-ization in Western Europe would be the consideration of ideological infection. Even if they were cowed and submissive, West European societies would pose a potentially mortal threat to the effectiveness of the KGB control apparatus over Soviet domestic life. It is possible that Soviet officials would find satisfactory solutions to the problem of controlling East-West person-to-person contacts, even in a "Finlandized" (or, more likely, worse) Europe; but the danger would be of major proportions.

Geopolitical thinking at the level of grand theory may easily lead its scholarly protagonists astray. For example, so much may be explained, though in so vague and general a way, that nothing in particular is illuminated; theories that purport to explain everything have a tendency to explain nothing in ways that are testable; reality *may* be described, but the human policymaker may be acting in ignorance of the precepts of the theorists; and, finally, it is an occupational hazard for the theorist who seeks to chart the shape of the woods that from time to time he will walk into a tree! Having registered those cautionary thoughts, the case for a geopolitical overview of East-West relations remains a strong one. Stated most succinctly, there is great merit in General Atkeson's contention that a major long-term Soviet policy goal is "hemispheric denial."[21] Ignoring the details for the moment, Soviet leaders aspire to deny the United States access to the World-Island of Eurasia. Although the preferred means for the attainment of such hegemony are undoubtedly nonmilitary, the Soviet armed forces are being modernized to the point that the United States would have to fight very hard indeed to enforce access to the Eurasian Rimlands. Soviet motives must, to a degree, remain unknown; but there is no need for speculation over the character of the military options that are being purchased.[22]

Unfortunately, one cannot have confidence that the United States will not, perhaps unwittingly, cooperate in a Soviet design for hemispheric

[21] Edward B. Atkeson, "Hemispheric Denial: Geopolitical Imperatives and Soviet Strategy," *Strategic Review,* vol. 4, no. 2 (Spring 1976), pp. 26-36.
[22] An excellent semipopular presentation of the pertinent military facts is *The Soviet War Machine, An Encyclopaedia of Russian Military Equipment and Strategy* (New York: Chartwell, 1976).

denial. Through want of will, or want of geopolitical education, the United States is likely to tire of the costs and immediate risks of its forward-deployed security connection with NATO-Europe long before the Heartland power of the Soviet Union reneges on its historic mission of achieving hegemony over all of Eurasia.[23] A *Festung Amerika* might survive, physically, in a world wherein Eurasia-Africa was organized according to the self-estimated security interests of the Soviet Union; but such an America would be very different, in adverse ways, from the America of today.

In short, as Sir Halford Mackinder and Nicholas Spykman explained in theory,[24] and as American politicians thus far have acknowledged by their deeds, denial of Soviet hegemony over the Eurasian Rimlands is a vital security interest of the United States. There is nothing crassly mechanistic about this proposition. It is not suggested here that *every* Rimland position is of vital importance. But the unifying concept of a long-term Soviet ambition for herispheric denial does serve usefully to undermine the basis of some of the arguments advanced by those who prefer to examine every clash of Soviet and American interests as being solely of local significance (if of any significance at all). A truly isolated defeat for American policy in, say, Angola, could not unreasonably be dismissed with some comment to the effect that "you win some and you lose some." But the significance of developments in Angola takes on a different aspect when those developments are set alongside the facts that an extreme Marxist clique has come to power in Mozambique, and that the Soviet Union has acquired air and naval facilities in Guinea and Somalia.

Considered in isolation, most local defeats can be rationalized. But the cumulative effect of developments favorable to the Soviet projection of military power all around the Rimlands of Eurasia-Africa must be greatly to facilitate the denial of access to the World-Island by American military power. (To deny such access, the Soviet Union does not need to control, or to be granted bases or military facilities in, every—or even most—Rimland countries.) Moreover, aside from the military consequences of Soviet success-by-proxy in countries bordering the South Atlantic and the Indian Ocean, there is a perceived political momentum to the Western retreat which raises expectations of Western acquiescence *next time*. To risk a statement of the obvious, a process of retreat is very difficult to arrest. If the United States tolerated North Vietnamese violations of the Paris Accords on a massive scale, leading to a fairly straightforward, old-fashioned invasion, and

---

[23] I have developed this theme in *The United States and Western Europe: Security Questions, Old and New* (Croton-on-Hudson, N.Y.: Hudson Institute, November 1976).

[24] See below.

declined to support its (admittedly unsavory) "friends" in Angola, why should the world at large believe that there is some forward ditch that the United States really would defend with whatever means were necessary?

Very many people in the United States and abroad hold to geopolitical conceptions that are inappropriate. In short, the wisdom that may be gleaned from the better geopolitical writings has no permanent, assured place in the American understanding of what it must do to ensure its security. It is probably more likely than not that the American polity will be persuaded, in the 1990s say, that its military commitment in Europe and in Eupropean waters is extraordinary and should be replaced, functionally, by an in-theater balance of power. Indeed, as a prediction rather than an aspiration, this author foresees a situation wherein NATO-Europe confronts a simple choice: endeavor to construct a strictly local balance as best it can (in the hope of providing some substantial political leverage *vis-à-vis* Soviet power), or come to the best terms available with the Soviet Union. This choice may seem unduly dramatic; but readers should remember that the forward American military commitment in and about Europe has always been explained to the American electorate as temporary. The American forward deployment is in Europe pending the evolution of a Western Europe capable of looking after itself. No American Administration has said to its electorate that the United States could not tolerate, on the grounds of the most basic self-interest, the domination of Eurasia by Soviet power; and that, therefore, Americans should think of their forward NATO commitment as a *permanent* investment.

American Presidents dare not admit publicly to the convictions that Western Europe will never (that is to say, in any foreseeable, even remotely policy-relevant future) be able to contain Soviet power by its own unaided efforts, or that the present disunited state of Western Europe really serves vital American interests better than would the United States of Europe that persists as a *desideratum* of American foreign policy. A United States of Europe, in American perspective, might fail to hold the "Rimland Dike" against Soviet pressures.[25] Also, its emergence—or even the serious prospect of its emergence—might provoke Soviet military action. It is a very distinct possibility that such a United States of Europe would provide the worst of all worlds for the United States. It would be sufficiently strong as to be able to resist American influence, and sufficiently strong (in prospect, at least) so as to speak eloquently to Soviet anxieties, and hence encourage Soviet intervention, but yet be too weak to resist Soviet pressure or overt military action. The most perceptive of American geopolitical thinkers,

---

[25] The term "Rimland" is Spykman's. See *The Geography of the Peace*, pp. 37-38, 40-41.

Nicholas Spykman, feared that the European Rimland might be so organized that it would threaten an imbalance of power on the World-Island that would be contrary to American interests.[26] A more likely danger is that Americans, tiring of "Cold War" commitments, will leave the European Rimland to fend for itself as best it is able. Spykman did not foresee the rise of the Soviet Union to a superpower category that would not be shared by any one, or combination, of Rimland powers.

The Theorists

Geopolitics must be distinguished from *Geopolitik*. Studies in the former category constitute what today tends to be termed policy science—that is, they seek to explore the structure of policy problems, without necessarily prescribing (let alone rationalizing) particular courses of policy action.[27] *Geopolitik,* by contrast, refers to the vast body of German geopolitical writing and "magic" cartography which flourished from the early 1920s until the demise of the Third Reich. It drew very freely upon the scholarly research and speculation of respectable, and respected, geopolitical thinkers outside of Germany, but its motive force was propagandistic. Major General Professor Doktor Karl Haushofer, the leading practitioner of *Geopolitik,* and his associates at the *Institut für Geopolitik* in Munich, provided pseudo-scientific rationales (the plural is used deliberately; *Geopolitik* did not permit considerations of consistency to interfere with the propaganda needs of the moment) for Germany's bid for world conquest.

American scholars in the very early 1940s took *Geopolitik* far too seriously, almost at its own evaluation. For example, in a book published in 1942, Robert Strausz-Hupé offered the opinion that "geopolitics is the master plan that tells what and why to conquer, guiding the military strategist along the easiest path to conquest. Thus the key to Hitler's global mind is German geopolitics."[28] The evidence for this sweeping claim was strictly circumstantial. Haushofer may have encouraged Hitler's dreams of conquest, but he cannot be held accountable for the course of German policy. Events provided the best commentary upon exaggerated American estimates of the importance of *Geopolitik*. In 1944, Karl Haushofer was consigned to the Dachau concentration camp and his son executed because of his supposed connection with the army officers responsible for the July bomb plot.

---

[26] *Ibid.*
[27] See Alexander L. George and Richard Smoke, *Deterrence in American Foreign Policy, Theory and Practice* (New York: Columbia University Press, 1974), Appendix.
[28] Strausz-Hupé, *op. cit.,* p. vii.

Geopolitik has significance for this study in two respects. First, it serves to demonstrate how geopolitical grand theory (however confused and internally contradictory) lends itself to abuse; and second, it tainted—in the minds of many people—all explicitly and self-avowedly geopolitical scholarship. A minor, but still important, claim of this study is to the effect that although geopolitics may never recover fully from the excesses of Haushofer and his *confrères,* all people everywhere frame their thoughts on foreign and defense policy within a (tacit) geopolitical framework.

Not merely does geography, understood broadly, very substantially influence the kind of people that we are and the character of our society; but in addition, our deeply sensed appreciation of where we belong provides critical guidance to how we react to "foreign" events. Natives of London, New York, and Tokyo carry around in their minds maps of the world that center, respectively, on London, New York, or Tokyo. If geopolitical study accomplishes nothing else, it does at least demonstrate very clearly that different maps carry different implications. Geopolitics may be out of fashion, but distinctive (political) interpretations of a common global geographical reality have a major, though often elusive, effect upon how we define problems (and what are defined as problems).

The raw materials for geopolitical theory, and the basic alternative syntheses, were assembled in a handful of pioneering works published at the close of the 19th century and during the first two decades of the 20th. The principal founders of geopolitics were Alfred Thayer Mahan, the American historian of British naval strategy, and advocate of sea power as *the* path to national greatness; Friedrich Ratzel, the founding father of modern political geography; Sir Halford Mackinder, the British geographer and politician; Sir James Fairgrieve, the British geographer who elaborated upon Mackinder's somewhat bare schematic theses; and Rudolf Kjellen, the Swedish geographer and enthusiast for the self-realization of pan-Germanic destiny. Of a later generation, Nicholas Spykman, an American professor of international relations, also merits mention, although as much for his insight into the enduring quality of international politics as for his specifically geopolitical theses. The theorists of (global) air power, in the opinion of this author, offered a *cul de sac.* The geopolitical hypotheses of, say, Alexander de Seversky have not—unlike those of Mackinder and Spykman—proven to be of lasting value, nor do they offer insights of policy relevance today. This, it must be added, is not to deprecate air power in its many facets.[29]

---

[29] A useful brief survey of the grander ideas of air power is offered in Edward Warner, "Douhet, Mitchell, Seversky: Theories of Air Warfare," in Earle, *op. cit.,* ch. 20. No less useful is Stephen B. Jones, "Global Strategic Views," *Geographical Review,* vol. 45, no. 4 (July 1955), pp. 492-508.

Without doubt the most influential and perceptive geopolitical thinker was Sir Halford Mackinder. Unfortunately, many of his critics and admirers both neglected the evolution of his views (his explicitly geopolitical writings span the period 1904-43!) and vulgarized, and even perverted, his arguments. As with most great conceptions, Mackinder's basic theses were of a devastating simplicity (rather like Mahan's ''discovery'' of sea power). The basic idea is that while Eurasia was for centuries properly considered a promontory, as a consequence of the greater efficiency of sea as opposed to overland communication and the impenetrability of the Arctic Ocean, the railroad revolution of the late 19th century foreshadowed such a change in the comparative advantage of land over sea communication that Eurasia-Africa should properly be considered a vast two-continent ''World-Island.''[30] The alleged comparative ease of land as opposed to sea transport (in the railroad age) is of fundamental importance to geopolitical theory. Mackinder observed, in 1904, that there is what he termed a Pivot Area in Eurasia which is inaccessible to sea power. This Pivot Area was defined, initially, as that region where the rivers drain into the ice-bound Arctic Ocean or into inland seas (the Caspian and the Aral).[31] Just as the Pivot Area was beyond the reach of (British) sea power, so the sea powers of his Outer Crescent (Great Britain, Japan, the United States) were invulnerable to the direct application of land power. But Mackinder predicted that the coming of railroads, and eventually air routes, within the Pivot Area of the World-Island, would alter the power relation between sea power and land power to the disadvantage of the former. Above all else, Mackinder feared that one or a combination of powers (Russia-Germany in particular) would utilize the new means of rapid overland communication, first, to create a vast imbalance of power in Eurasia, then to conquer the Eurasian World-Island, and eventually to utilize the resources of the World-Island in a bid for world conquest. He foresaw that such a bid, on the basis of the rival resource bases of the World-Island and the Outer Crescent, would succeed.

In his major work, *Democratic Ideals and Reality,* published in 1919, Mackinder redefined his Pivot Area along more expansive lines, and he borrowed the felicitous term Heartland from Sir James Fairgrieve.[32] But the basic opposition was the same—land power, which he held to have a growing advantage, versus sea power. Mackinder was not deterministic, nor was he an apostle of world conquest or of brutal *realpolitik*. Contrary to a

---

[30] The most important of Mackinder's geopolitical writings are collected in the volume *Democratic Ideals and Reality* (New York: Norton, 1962). This book offers the title manuscript (first published in 1919) and three very important additional articles.

[31] See ''The Geographical Pivot of History,'' in *ibid.*, pp. 241-264.

[32] *Democratic Ideals and Reality*, ch. 4.

Map One

The Natural Seats of Power

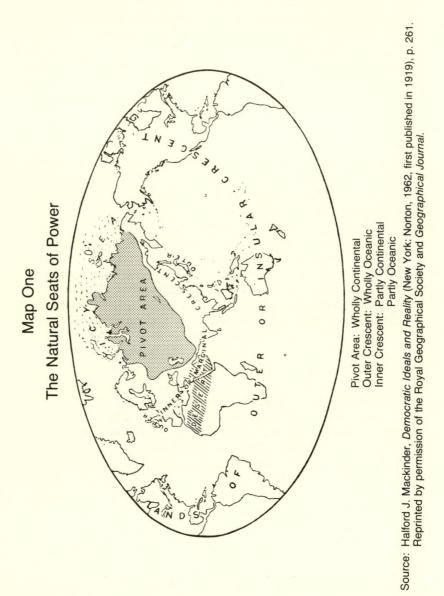

Pivot Area: Wholly Continental
Outer Crescent: Wholly Oceanic
Inner Crescent: Partly Continental
                  Partly Oceanic

Source: Halford J. Mackinder, *Democratic Ideals and Reality* (New York: Norton, 1962, first published in 1919), p. 261.
         Reprinted by permission of the Royal Geographical Society and *Geographical Journal.*

popular image of geopolitics, this leading theorist in the genre was profoundly humane in his motives, which were as different from those of the semimystical creed of *Geopolitik* as could be imagined.[33] Mackinder did not claim that land power, in the form of one power or a tight axis of powers, *must* come to dominate the World-Island (or Great Continent as he sometimes preferred to call Eurasia), and hence the world. Rather did he claim that "the grouping of lands and seas, and of fertility and natural pathways, is such as to lend itself to the growth of empires, and in the end of a single world-empire."[34] He foresaw a danger (to Britain in particular, his primary concern), not an inevitability; the insular powers of the Outer Crescent, in support of countries on the Inner Crescent, should therefore seek to ensure that no single power or alliance came to control all of the resources of the World-Island.

As one would expect, the details of Mackinder's theory altered as circumstances changed. By 1943, he had left far behind the notion of a Heartland defined in terms of Arctic Ocean and continental river drainage. Instead, he claimed that "for our present purpose, it is sufficiently accurate to say that the territory of the USSR is equivalent to the Heartland."[35] In the same article, he offered the following warning:[36]

All things considered, the conclusion is unavoidable that if the Soviet Union emerges from this war as conquerer of Germany, she must rank as the greatest land power on the globe. Moreover, she will be the power in the strategically strongest defensive position. The Heartland is the greatest natural fortress on earth. For the first time in history, it is manned by a garrison sufficient both in number and quality.

It is paradoxical that Mackinder's world view was focused, in its formative years, upon a posited fundamental rivalry between British sea power and Russian land power—a focus entirely natural to a British writer prior to 1907 (the year of the Anglo-Russian entente). Mackinder predicted that the ocean highways of the world, the interior lines of communication of the British Empire, were about to be overtaken in relative strategic advantage by a railroad age in, and leading from, the Heartland. In short, Russia would enjoy superior access to the keys to British overseas wealth and influence around the Inner Crescent. Leaving aside for the moment some technical weaknesses in Mackinder's theory, the paradox was that *the*

---

[33] See *ibid.*, ch. 6-7.
[34] *Ibid.*, p. 2.
[35] "The Round World and the Winning of the Peace," in *ibid.*, p. 269.
[36] *Ibid.*, pp. 272-273.

Map Two

Mackinder's Development of the Heartland

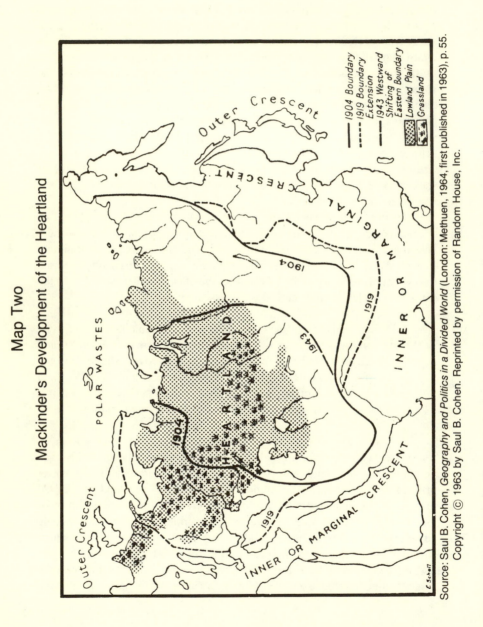

Source: Saul B. Cohen, *Geography and Politics in a Divided World* (London: Methuen, 1964, first published in 1963), p. 55.
Copyright © 1963 by Saul B. Cohen. Reprinted by permission of Random House, Inc.

danger to British power until the early 1940s did not stem from a dynamic and aggressive Eurasian Heartland, but rather from the vulnerability of that Heartland to conquest by peninsular-European Germany. Mackinder did, of course, recognize this variation upon his early scenario. Indeed, in 1919 he urged most forcefully the construction of a tier of states in Eastern Europe that could serve as a strong buffer zone for the protection of the Soviet Republic against a German attempt to control the Heartland. It was in this context that Mackinder coined his famous dictum:[37]

> *Who rules East Europe commands the Heartland:*
> *Who rules the Heartland commands the World-Island:*
> *Who rules the World-Island commands the World.*

Mackinder was wrong; he had too little faith in the robustness of his own conception. In 1941-43, Nazi Germany not only ruled East Europe, its armies stood on the banks of the Volga at the gateway to Asia—and yet the Heartland power recovered and secured total victory. By 1943, Mackinder *de facto* acknowledged the frailty of the dictum quoted above, for he sketched, though only in barest detail, the thesis that a North Atlantic region could balance the threat that might be posed by the Soviet Union after the defeat of Germany. Mackinder pointed to the development of a second "embankment of power," embracing America, Britain, and France (as its cores). In his words:[38]

> . . . My second [the first was the Heartland] geographical concept, that of the Midland Ocean—the North Atlantic—and its dependent seas and river basins. Without laboring the details of that concept, let me picture it again in its three elements—a bridgehead in France, a moated aerodrome in Britain, and a reserve of trained manpower, agriculture, and industries in the eastern United States and Canada. So far as war potential goes, both the United States and Canada are Atlantic countries, and since instant land warfare is in view, both the bridgehead and the moated aerodrome are essential to amphibious power.

Pride of place has been given to the theories of Halford Mackinder because this author judges his conceptions to be of the greatest inherent interest, the most relevant to contemporary policy, and to have been the most influential. Mahan's writings on sea power are often contrasted with the land

---

[37] *Democratic Ideals and Reality*, p. 150.
[38] "The Round World and the Winning of the Peace," in *ibid.*, p. 277.

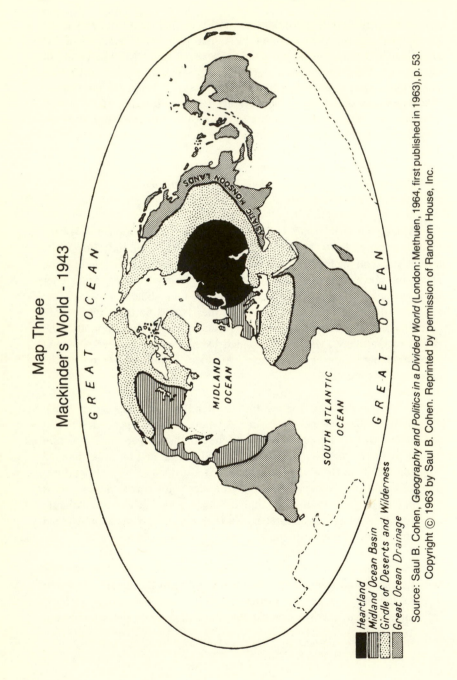

Map Three
Mackinder's World - 1943

Heartland
Midland Ocean Basin
Girdle of Deserts and Wilderness
Great Ocean Drainage

Source: Saul B. Cohen, *Geography and Politics in a Divided World* (London: Methuen, 1964, first published in 1963), p. 53.

power orientation of Mackinder. Such an opposition is largely misleading. Mackinder did not challenge Mahan's argument that British power and influence in the world was substantially a consequence of the rise of British sea power. But Mackinder did claim that Mahan greatly underrated the importance of the geography of the British Isles as a secure, indeed well-nigh impregnable, base for the development and exercise of sea power. Furthermore, Mackinder argued that because of the coming of railroads and air routes, fewer and fewer of Britain's naval bases and facilities around the littoral of the Eurasian World-Island would have secure hinterlands, and that more and more of the great ocean highways would come to warrant description as "closed seas," dominated by land power (and land-based air power). But the most important of Mackinder's arguments *vis-à-vis* Mahan and lesser sea power enthusiasts (apart from the crucial claim that the revolution in transport technology had changed the comparative advantage of land as opposed to sea communications) was that dominant land power in the World-Island would permit the development of dominant sea power: the Heartland power or powers would have the resource potential to overwhelm the formerly insular powers *in their own element.*[39]

Writing in the early 1940s, an American political scientist, Nicholas Spykman, took over the geographical elements of Mackinder's theory and offered a strong critique that rested upon the historical facts of the first half of the 20th century. Spykman was highly critical of Mackinder's *leitmotiv* of the opposition between British sea power and Russian land power. Spykman reminded his readers that World Wars I and II were not simple land power-sea power struggles. Furthermore, Spykman was not convinced that Mackinder's Heartland (which Spykman—with Mackinder—interpreted, correctly as of 1942, as being effectively coterminous with the Soviet Union) had the potential, in the foreseeable future, to make the predicted bid for control of the World-Island.[40] Indeed, Spykman boldly offered a counterdictum to that offered by Mackinder in his 1919 book.[41]

Who controls the rimland rules Eurasia; who rules Eurasia controls the destinies of the world.

Spykman observed that the United States had twice this century entered a World War in order to prevent the domination of the Eurasian (essentially

---

[39] Claims for the superiority of sea power over land power have recently been revived in sweeping terms in Robert E. Walters, *The Nuclear Trap, An Escape Route* (London: Penguin, 1974). This book is noteworthy for the attention that it pays to geopolitical concepts.

[40] Spykman's *magnum opus* was *America's Strategy in World Politics*, cited above.

[41] *The Geography of the Peace*, p. 43.

Map Four
The World of Spykman

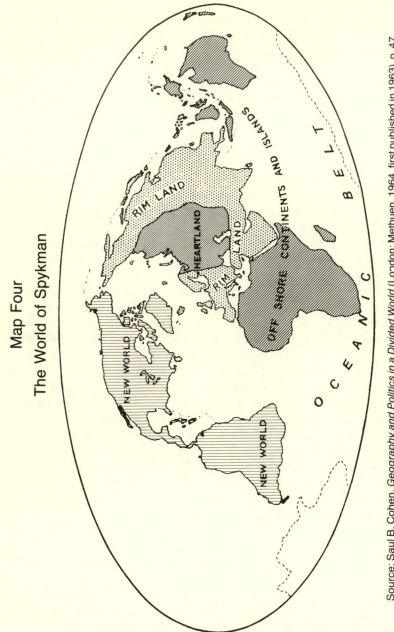

Source: Saul B. Cohen, *Geography and Politics in a Divided World* (London: Methuen, 1964, first published in 1963), p. 47.
Copyright © 1963 by Saul B. Cohen. Reprinted by permission of Random House, Inc.

European and, in 1941, East Asian also) Rimlands by a single power. In short, Spykman did not challenge the fundamental thesis of Mackinder, that maintenance of a balance of power on the World-Island was essential to the security of insular powers; rather did he disagree as to the potential strength of the Eurasian Rimlands—if organized by a single power or axis—*vis-à-vis* the Eurasian Heartland. Spykman must be judged to have overestimated the resisting power of the Eurasian Rimlands and to have underestimated the power potential of the Soviet Union. But looking at the world of the late 1970s, the theories of Mackinder and Spykman yield a common logic for policy. The United States cannot afford to tolerate the effective control of Eurasia-Africa by the Soviet Union. It must serve, in its own vital interests, as the functional successor to Great Britain as an active balancer of power on, and bearing upon, the Rimlands of Eurasia. Such a geopolitical task is as essential as it should—given steadiness of purpose and an appropriate popular understanding of that purpose—be successful.

Whereas Mackinder and Spykman saw geopolitical analysis as a tool for the framing of prudent balance of power policies intended to maintain an effective equilibrium of opposing power centers in and relating to Eurasia-Africa, the German school of *Geopolitik* expanded the writ of the ideas of Ratzel, Mackinder, and Kjellen (in particular) into a license for attempted world conquest.[42] *Geopolitik* went beyond Mackinder's contention that mastery of Eurasia meant eventual mastery of the world. Haushofer and his followers advocated very actively that Germany seek such mastery. States were held to be living organisms that expand or contract as they struggle more or less successfully with other states. War was believed to be the normal condition of interstate relations, with frontiers expressing the temporary, current balance of power. In Haushofer's words: "Boundaries are fighting places rather than legal norms of division."[43] In practice, *Geopolitik* and Nazi expansionist propaganda melded virtually beyond separability. Haushofer preached economic autarky, and presented more a series of catchwords and phrases in service of the proposition that it was Germany's manifest destiny to dominate Eurasia (as the first step: the destruction of British and American sea power) than he did a rigorous system of thought. Key terms in the litany of *Geopolitik* were *Blut und Boden* (race and land/soil), *Raum und Lage* (area and location), *Macht und Raum* (power and area), and of course *Lebensraum* (living space). To his credit, Haushofer was not enthusiastic over the prospect of war with the Soviet

---

[42] The contributions of Ratzel, Mackinder, and Kjellen to *Geopolitik* are explained in Whittlesey, *German Strategy of World Conquest*, and Strausz-Hupé, *op. cit.*
[43] Quoted in Whittlesey, *German Strategy of World Conquest*, p. 73.

Map Five
Magic Geography

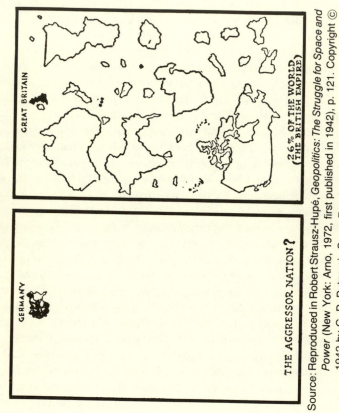

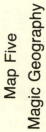

Source: Reproduced in Robert Strausz-Hupé, *Geopolitics: The Struggle for Space and Power* (New York: Arno, 1972, first published in 1942), p. 121. Copyright © 1942 by G. P. Putnam's Sons. Reprinted by permission.

Union. Indeed, the practitioners of *Geopolitik* long advocated alliance with the Heartland power (and Japan also, if possible)—though naturally with Germany as the senior partner.

Geopolitics Today

Flawed conceptions are easy to identify with the advantage of retrospective knowledge. Mackinder's notion that the future would be shaped by the opposition between sea power and land power has looked better and better as time separates us from World War II. It is little short of remarkable that his theory should be so robust, given the facts that two of its critical inspiring ideas are false. Specifically, despite heroic efforts (in good part expended by slave labor) to develop western Siberia, the Pivot Area or Heartland identified by Mackinder in 1904 does not, even today, begin to approach the condition predicted. Rail links in Siberia continue to be few. With the sole, though major, exception of the East European gateway, the Soviet Union would have enormous difficulty projecting power into the Rimlands of Eurasia—depending on those land routes foreseen by Mackinder as the interior lines of the Heartland power. In part as a consequence, Mackinder was not correct (save with respect to peninsular Europe) in claiming that land power had inherent, and growing, advantage over sea power. In his very important study, "Illusions of Distance," Albert Wohlstetter demonstrated convincingly that, notwithstanding transoceanic distances, the United States could transport men and material more cheaply to the southern and eastern littorals of Eurasia than could the Heartland power.[44] In addition, geography considered as mere distance is today an irrelevance to the efficiency with which electronic communication can be conducted. Unfortunately, Wohlstetter's persuasive arguments do not tell the entire story. If they did, then Mahan's idea of the inherent superiority of Anglo-American sea power (and air power, to modernize the argument) would invalidate the grand conception of Mackinder.

It should be recalled that a critical feature in Mackinder's theory was the idea of the invulnerability of the continental and insular citadels of land power and sea power to direct action one against the other. Long-range aircraft and ballistic missiles of intercontinental reach have changed that condition forever. But the very totality with which mutual vulnerability has emerged has served to minimize its significance. The maritime alliance of Mackinder's Midland Ocean (NATO) can, in principle, seek to defend its Eurasian Rimland interests by threatening direct action against the Soviet Heartland. But the Soviet Union has, since the mid-1960s, constructed a

---

[44] *Foreign Affairs*, vol. 46, no. 2 (January 1968), pp. 242-255.

strategic nuclear counterdeterrent that promises, on current trends, to preserve the inviolability of the Heartland fortress.

Some critics have charged Mackinder with propagating a myth in his idea of the essential unity of the World-Island. Until the present day, there has been much to recommend the judgment that the concept of the World-Island is little more than a geographer's conceit. However, Soviet policy over the past decade, particularly with respect to the forging of a nascent "security system," is beginning to change a conceit into a possible, even probable, reality. Soviet real-time control over the policies of all states in Eurasia-Africa is a very distant prospect indeed. On the other hand, the Soviet Union does not need to accomplish such a difficult task in order to secure for itself predominance over the World-Island, and the ability to deny American access.

3

Geopolitics and Soviet Power: Breaking Out of the Heartland

For a thousand years, a series of horse-riding peoples emerged from Asia through the broad interval between the Ural Mountains and the Caspian Sea, rode through the open spaces of southern Russia, and struck home into Hungary in the very heart of the European peninsula, shaping by the necessity of opposing them the history of each of the great peoples around.[45]

Geography, History, Opportunity

Distinctive political culture, which substantially determines national *style* in foreign and military affairs, is the product of a distinctive national historical experience—and that distinctive national historical experience reflects no less distinctive a blend of national geographical conditions. Western policymakers today, seeking to understand Soviet behavior and to divine Soviet intentions, have a large repository of enlightening historical data upon which to draw, should they so choose. The Iron Law of Triviality, to which reference was made in Chapter 1, applies to Western officials no less than to Western scholars. Those officials tend to be well-briefed on the singular characteristics of the Kiev-class antisubmarine cruiser/aircraft carrier, and on the probable ballistic coefficients of Soviet re-entry vehicles; but the nature of the Soviet adversary and "what it is about," in long-term perspective, are subjects that do not emerge in the day-by-day round of policymaking.

From the perspective of long-term Western security interests, the Revolution of 1917 was of little importance. The Soviet Union has been

---

[45] Mackinder, "The Geographical Pivot of History," *loc. cit.*, pp. 249-250.

governed in a style wholly Russian, and its foreign and defense policy behavior would appear to owe very little indeed to the inspiration offered by ideological texts. The revolutionary clique which inherited the Tsarist state shared the same distinctively Russian attitudes towards political affairs as did their aristocratic predecessors, and naturally they inherited the same set of geopolitical problems and opportunities. The disciples of detente in the United States, thinned though their ranks appear to be, need to appreciate that in dealing with the Soviet Union the West is dealing with what Richard Pipes has termed a "patrimonial" state—that is to say, a state wherein the "citizens" (to stretch terminology) and their labor are the property of the rulers.[46]

> A despot violates his subjects' property rights; a patrimonial ruler does not even acknowledge their existence . . . In a patrimonial state, there exist no formal limitations on political authority, nor rule of law, nor individual liberties.

The precise historical roots of patrimonialism in Russia are not important to the theme of this study; but what is important is the fact that this inherently illiberal condition is no recent invention. It stems from Russian history, which was the product of the interplay of particular geopolitical factors. The conquest of the black earth belt of the steppe, and later of the entire Eurasian Heartland, by a state that had its origins in the northern taiga must be explained in terms of reactions to physical geography, rather than imperialistic impulses. Russian history is a story of continuous colonization; in the words of a celebrated Russian historian, "the history of Russia is the history of a country which colonizes itself."[47] The northern location of the country, the extreme continental climate, and the poverty of the soil of the taiga required a process of continuous colonial expansion into the fertile steppelands that either were held strongly by nomadic khanates of Central Asian origin, or were held/coveted by the major military powers of Lithuania-Poland and the Teutonic Knights. In short, Russian farming expansion into fertile regions required constant military protection. As many historians have noted, the major reason why Russian expansion southwards, southwestwards, and southeastwards, and eventually due east to the Pacific littoral of Siberia, was never reversed significantly, was because the Russian

[46] Richard Pipes, *Russia Under the Old Regime* (New York: Scribner, 1974), p. 23. Pipes' excellent book may usefully be supplemented by Tibor Szamuely, *The Russian Tradition*, edited and introduced by Robert Conquest (New York: McGraw-Hill, 1974).
[47] V.O. Kliuchevskii, quoted in Pipes, *op. cit.*, p. 14.

political-military *imperium* was paralleled fairly closely by Russian colonization. Russia conquered the Eurasian Heartland as a consequence of the
military necessity to protect its dynamic agricultural frontier from depre-
dation by steppe raiders.

It is just possible that there may be some people in the West who believe
some mix of the following claims: that the alleged Soviet will to expand
(either crudely by territorial grab, or more subtly through some variant of
"Findlandization") is a myth (the acquisitions of the period 1939-45 were
clearly defensively motivated, as is the security system of the Warsaw Pact);
that the period 1945-49 was an "extraordinary" one, dominated by
circumstances (opportunities!) and by a personality extremely unlikely to
recur; and overall, that the geopolitical situation of the Soviet Union, as
interpreted by Soviet officials, is really one of acute vulnerability (hence, the
Soviet "threat" to establish hegemony over Eurasia is the natural reaction of
a beleaguered garrison endeavoring to conduct an aggressive defense). In
historical perspective, these claims and their variants are simply wrong. In
one major respect, this line of reasoning might just be correct; but no comfort
can be drawn therefrom by Western observers. Specifically, it is possible
that the Soviet threat to the Eurasian Rimlands is an expression of fear rather
than of a determination by the Soviet Union to pursue a manifest destiny of
expanding power and influence. But if this thought has any merit, it should
be balanced by the realization that Soviet paranoia (on the scale reflected in
the military build-up and modernization programs of the 1960s and 1970s) is
no less dangerous to Western (and Eastern) countries than would be a will to
power for the sake of power. A quest for *absolute* security must lead a
country on the path of world conquest.

Territorial expansion was "the Russian way," just as it has been "the
Soviet way." Richard Pipes reminds us that it is estimated, for example, that
between the middle of the 16th century and the end of the 17th, Russia
conquered territory the size of the modern Netherlands *every year* for *150
years* running."[48] Furthermore, unlike the case of most other imperial
powers, conquest by Russia became a permanent and nonnegotiable
political fact (save under conditions of extreme duress, as with the Treaty of
Brest-Litovsk in March 1918). The territorial growth of a state over a
500-year period cannot neatly and simply be ascribed to a single impulse. It
is sufficient for the purposes of this study that the process of expansion be
noted, and that certain features of that expansion be duly registered for their
possible relevance to current and future policy.

---

[48] "Detente: Moscow's View," in Richard Pipes, ed., *Soviet Strategy in Europe* (New York:
Crane, Russak, 1976), p. 9. Emphasis in the original.

As George Kennan observed in 1946, Russia/USSR has had, and has, no notion of "good neighborliness" or of stable political lines of demarcation.[49] The Russian state, unlike insular Britain or a United States bordered by weak and (eventually) fundamentally "friendly" countries, has always abutted potentially hostile powers. The natural enmity of neighbors is a precept for Russians that stems very directly from long historical experience—and it is an inherited view which Anglo-Saxons (though not Germans or Frenchmen) have some considerable difficulty in appreciating. To repeat, slightly rephrased, the complex aphorism with which this chapter began: foreign and defense policy are substantially determined by political culture, and political culture is very largely the product of national historical experience, which—in its turn—reflects evolving national geographical circumstances. Russian/Soviet history is a story of wars, literally, for physical survival (Khazar horsemen or the *Waffen SS*—the essential story is the same). Russian history attests to the truth of Haushofer's claim that "boundaries are fighting places."[50] This fairly obvious observation on the Russian/Soviet historical experience is not advanced as an excuse for recent Soviet outward pressure, but it is a fact of Russian history which we would do well to remember when attempts are made to understand the outlook of Soviet officials. Their Soviet Socialist duty is to redouble the struggle against the objective enemies of socialism, while their Russian inheritance tells them that peace is simply a period of preparation for future war. This inheritance is, of course, far from uniquely Russian. It is, however, totally alien to liberal optimistic thought in the West in general and in the United States in particular. American readers of this study may not care for this judgment, but it is difficult to resist the thought that the United States is, by some margin, the country least well-fitted by political culture to be charged with a major power-balancing role *vis-à-vis* the Soviet Union. This judgment is backhanded praise. Many of the virtues of the United States translate into vices when it comes to the practice of international politics.

From its original base in the taiga of northern Europe, Russia/USSR has expanded territorially when and where it could. This process of expansion may be explained by a mix of the following impulses: domestic economic necessity; specific security concerns; and a hard-earned empathy for the brutal facts of international political life. Physical geography did not bequeath to the Russian state natural protection from hostile forces to the west, the south, or the east. Indeed, for several centuries the only refuge for Russian farmers was the forest. Once Russian colonists ventured in numbers

---

[49] *Memoirs, 1925-1950* (London: Hutchinson, 1968, first published 1967), pp. 560-561.
[50] See fn. 43.

onto the open steppe (which stretches from Hungary to Mongolia!), the safety of the southern marches could rest only upon Russian military power and a combination of vast defensive depth and a very rigorous climate. European Russia has no land over 1,400 feet high. To the west was a 700-mile wide (*two-way*) gateway into peninsular Europe, between the Black Sea and the Baltic; while to the east there was a gateway between the southern limits of the Urals and the Caspian Sea. Depending upon the relative strength of the Russian state and its neighbors, these gateways were either dangerous invasion routes or highways for expansion.

There is an ambivalence in the geopolitical circumstances of the Russian/Soviet state which is fully reflected in the differing judgments of geopolitical theorists. The central location of the Heartland *vis-à-vis* the Rimlands permits a multiplicity of applied pressures around the periphery, but that central location also means accessibility from the Rimlands (and across the Arctic Ocean) at many points. Whether Russian/Soviet geography is a source of strength or weakness can be judged appropriately only in terms of the political-military conditions of the time in question.

Despite Mackinder's dire predictions in 1904, the fact remains that the Soviet geopolitical context relative to that of the Rimlands and the maritime alliance supportive of many Rimland states, is clearly advantageous *only in Europe*. In terms of power projection *from the Heartland*, the Soviet Union is at present (a vital qualification) probably at a disadvantage in the Far East and in Southeast Asia. The Soviet acquisition of military facilities bordering on, or easily accessible to, the Indian Ocean (for example, in Iraq), married to a growing local naval deployment, renders judgment concerning the Soviet-American balance in the Indian Ocean basin extremely uncertain. Unfortunately, the power-projection advantage yielded by the Soviet relationship to Western Europe might well suffice as the condition that could lead to hegemony over all of Eurasia-Africa. If Soviet leaders either acquire effective control over all of Western Europe, or even if they succeed in detaching what currently is organized as NATO-Europe from the American security system, then all things become possible for the Soviet Union.

Notwithstanding the judgment offered above concerning the pre-eminent importance of control of peninsular Europe for the fulfillment of Soviet ambitions, geopolitical relationships in the Far East have a long-term nightmarish quality to them for the Soviet Union. Both Mackinder and Spykman assigned China to the inner or marginal crescent, or Rimlands (see Maps Two and Four), for reasons that have become very obvious indeed over the past two decades. In order to control its Far Eastern, and even Central Asian, holdings, the Soviet Union needs a strong forward position in defense of the dual-track railroad lifeline of those holdings (the Trans-Siberian Railroad). The Inner Asian frontier zone that separates Soviet from Chinese power (in Manchuria, Mongolia, and Sinkiang) comprises continuous, virtually featureless steppes and desert to depths varying between 200 and 400 miles. The Trans-Siberian Railroad parallels the Sino-Soviet frontier along the Amur and Ussuri Rivers, while—in addition—for 800 miles it is less than 150 miles from the border of Mongolia. Soviet deployment of 43 divisions along the frontier zone abutting Chinese territory (including three in Mongolia) speaks to a justified anxiety. Chinese outward pressure, north and particularly northwestwards, is an historical fact born of long experience with threats from Central Asia (of which the Soviet is simply the latest manifestation). China's technological weakness and general lack of industrial development affords the Soviet Union a breathing space; but eventually, well over a billion Chinese must come to place at serious risk the entire Soviet position in the Far East.[51]

Careful study of Russian/Soviet geography, history, and (consequent) political culture should yield to American politicians and officials the following policy-relevant items for serious notice.

> 1. Soviet officials do not believe that power relations can, or should, be stabilized. Their ideology and their national history both direct them to a dynamic view of the "correlation of forces."
>
> 2. Expansion is the Russian/Soviet "way": the Pacific Ocean has been reached, but not (yet) the Atlantic. It is highly improbable that Soviet officials would ever be prepared to settle, prospectively permanently, for lines of political-military demarcation that fell short of encompassing the entire World-Island of Eurasia-Africa. The circumstances of the military *dénouement* to World War II meant that the rump of peninsular Europe not occupied by the Soviet Army would lack defensive depth in a future war.
>
> 3. The Soviet commitment to world dominion is nonnegotiable. American concepts of stability and order are contrary to the political basis of the Soviet state. In practice, the bureaucrats of the Communist Party of the Soviet Union may behave like the patrimonial aristocrats of the Old Regime, but those bureaucrats know that their only right to rule over the Heartland rests upon a theory which posits a deadly and inescapable struggle between the antagonistic social systems of socialism and capitalism/imperialism (and deviant socialism).

---

[51] See Clifton C. Carpenter, "The Inner Asian Frontier: A Cradle of Conflict," *Strategic Review*, vol. 5, no. 1 (Winter 1977), pp. 90-99.

4. The Russian/Soviet domestic and foreign historical experience has been marked by extreme brutality. The Russian and Soviet states sustained themselves by force. While military force is the *ultima ratio* of all regimes and governments, Soviet officials cannot be ignorant of the facts that Soviet power was established in Russia by force of arms; Soviet power was defended by force of arms in the critical period of War Communism and later in the Great Patriotic War; and that military power is the only index of interstate comparison on which the Soviet Union has registered a very marked success over recent decades.

Geopolitical factors appear to be propitious for the advancement of Soviet interests. Through the historical accident of the course of World War II, Soviet ground and air forces are deployed sufficiently far forward in Central Europe that a Blitzkrieg campaign against Western Europe should have excellent prospects of success. NATO's defense planners face many problems which, with intelligence and application, could be resolved. The one problem that is beyond solution, and which forecloses upon many conceivable defensive strategies, is NATO's lack of geographical depth. Military history shows that surprise Blitzkriegs tend to succeed—at least at first. To survive a Blitzkrieg, one needs to purchase time for recovery. NATO-Europe lacks territorial space that could be surrendered temporarily for recovery time. That reserve of trained manpower which Mackinder saw as being transferable across the Atlantic (the Midland Ocean) could not be transferred in sufficient numbers in time for it to affect the course of the campaign. Mackinder also insisted upon the retention of a bridgehead upon the European mainland; but 60 or 90 days into a war in Europe, how extensive would be the perimeter of the bridgehead of the maritime alliance in Europe?[52]

Geopolitical relations in Central Europe are a matter of major interest to this study, because—unlike the clashes of East-West interest elsewhere (save with respect to the Middle East, and the Persian Gulf in particular)—the achievement by the Soviet Union of hegemony over this region would, in and of itself, mean a decisive and immediate shift in the global balance of power. Even Soviet success in the Persian Gulf area would largely have meaning in terms of its effects upon the policies of European countries (and Japan). Two geopolitical "core" regions far removed from the demarcation lines in Central Europe also merit explicit attention for their direct relevance to the projection of Soviet power into and over the Marginal Seas of Eurasia

---

[52] Soviet forces in, and strategy concerning, Europe are very well described and analyzed in John Erickson, *Soviet-Warsaw Pact Force Levels* (Washington: United States Strategic Institute, 1976).

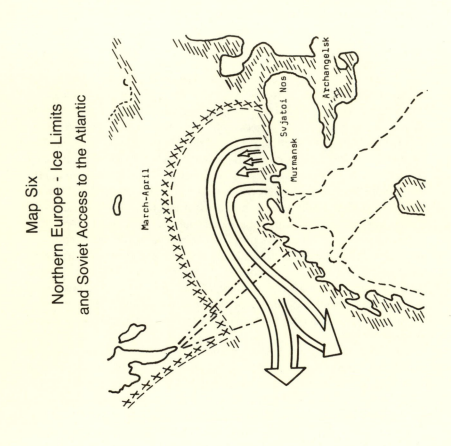

Map Six

Northern Europe - Ice Limits

and Soviet Access to the Atlantic

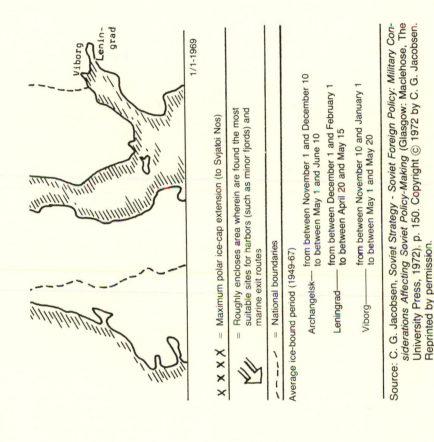

x x x x = Maximum polar ice-cap extension (to Svjatoi Nos)

= Roughly encloses area wherein are found the most
suitable sites for harbors (such as minor fjords) and
marine exit routes

- - - - = National boundaries

Average ice-bound period (1949-67)

Archangelsk—— from between November 1 and December 10
to between May 1 and June 10

Leningrad—— from between December 1 and February 1
to between April 20 and May 15

Viborg—— from between November 10 and January 1
to between May 1 and May 20

Source: C. G. Jacobsen, *Soviet Strategy - Soviet Foreign Policy: Military Con-
siderations Affecting Soviet Policy-Making* (Glasgow: Maclehose, The
University Press, 1972), p. 150. Copyright © 1972 by C. G. Jacobsen.
Reprinted by permission.

that the United States must control if it is to be assured of access to Rimland allies. Specifically, the Soviet Union has developed major complexes of military bases in the Kola Peninsula (centered upon the Kola Inlet itself and the port of Murmansk and the naval base and shipyards of Severomorsk) and in the Far East (with three principal base areas: Vladivostok, Sovietskaya Gavan, and Petropavlovsk).[53] The leading Western student of Soviet military affairs, John Erickson, has observed that "the greatest single concentration of military bases in the world is presently located on the Kola Peninsula."[54]

Described in offensive perspective, these two geopolitical core areas have significance for their utility in denying American sea power free access through North Atlantic and North Pacific waters. Soviet geography has dictated a quadripartite division of Soviet sea power. The four fleet base areas all have their distinctive limitations: the Baltic and Black Seas fleets are based in potentially "closed seas" (with the choke points at the Dardanelles, the Oresund Strait out of the Baltic, the Strait of Gibraltar, and the Suez Canal); while the Northern and Pacific fleets are not without their problems in terms of access to the open sea. The Kola coastline offers 240) miles, ice-free year-round (from the Norwegian frontier to Svjatoi Nos), while the mean southernmost distance of the icepack from the Kola coastline is 180 miles. Soviet surface vessels thus are restricted for part of the year by the narrow corridor between land and ice, and—all year round—they (and submarines also) must, for access into the North Atlantic, transit the NATO-monitored gateway into the North Atlantic, the Greenland-Iceland-Faeroes-United Kingdom gap(s).

Geography changes in its political meaning as a result of changes in the military capabilities of rival states (among other factors). In terms of political influence in "peacetime," and perhaps even military vulnerability in wartime, the Soviet military build-up of the past decade has changed the strategic meaning of the Kola Peninsula. Norway, Denmark, and possibly even Great Britain are today outflanked by the deployment of Soviet naval and naval air power from the Kola Peninsula. In a period of crisis, the Soviet Union could deploy task forces into the North and Norwegian Seas and into the North Atlantic (from Kola bases *and* from the Baltic); these task forces would have a major impact upon the deliberations of the NATO (and neutral) governments of Northern Europe. Western naval strategists are wont to talk

---

[53] The discussion which follows is heavily indebted to C.G. Jacobsen, *Soviet Strategy-Soviet Foreign Policy, Military Considerations Affecting Soviet Policy-Making* (Glasgow: Maclehose, The University Press, 1972), ch. 6.
[54] Erickson, *Soviet-Warsaw Pact Force Levels*, p. 72.

of the principal Western naval mission of *sea control* and the principal Soviet objective of effecting *sea denial*. These concepts, though useful, are also misleading. The Soviet Navy (and naval air force) is not strong enough to deny the North Atlantic to NATO shipping. But it is strong enough to compel NATO countries to wage a major campaign to ensure substantial freedom of movement of seaborne cargo. In a war for control of the European Rimland, the decisive interaction will be between Soviet-Warsaw Pact and NATO ground forces. The task of the Soviet Navy (as of Soviet frontal, or tactical, aviation) will be to do, and to prevent the infliction of, sufficient damage, so that the ground forces can occupy territory very expeditiously. The history of Soviet-Finnish relations from 1939 until 1944, and Soviet-Norwegian relations since 1945 attests to the major significance attached by Soviet officials to the Kola Peninsula. Kola is the base area for the largest Soviet fleet and is second in importance only to Central Europe as a geographical forward platform for the projection of military power.[55]

Of the three Soviet naval base complexes in the Far East, only one—Petropavlovsk in Kamchatka—has direct access to the open ocean. By reason of its natural harbor, inland communications, developed facilities, and tolerable ice and fog conditions, Vladivostok is the principal base for the Pacific fleet of the Soviet Union. But seaborne access to Vladivostok is through the Sea of Japan, and transit of all save the northernmost of the straits which lead into that sea (the Tartar Strait, between Sakhalin and the mainland) is easily monitored, and could be blocked by enemy forces based in the Japanese islands. Access to Vladivostok and Sovietskaya Gavan in a northerly direction entails transit of either the Tartar or La Perouse (between Sakhalin and Hokkaido) Straits: both straits lead into the Sea of Okhotsk. The physical geography of its Siberian littoral, with its offshore island chains, explains very clearly why the Soviet Union will never cede the Kurile Islands back to Japan. If the Kuriles were returned to Japan, the Japanese (or a hostile power using Japanese-provided facilities) could render the Sea of Okhotsk a "closed sea" to the Soviet Union. The major submarine base at Petropavlovsk, on the southeastern coast of Kamchatka, has manageable ice and fog problems, has no "closed sea" difficulties, and lies only 500 miles north of the main east-west shipping route of the North Pacific.

---

[55] The Soviet Navy and its missions have come to be popular subjects for analysis and speculation in the West. Useful studies include Norman Polmar, *Soviet Naval Power, Challenge for the 1970s,* rev. ed. (New York: Crane, Russak, 1974); Michael MccGwire, Ken Booth, and John McDonnell, eds., *Soviet Naval Policy, Objectives and Constraints* (New York: Praeger, 1975); and John E. Moore, *The Soviet Navy Today* (London: Macdonald and Janes, 1975).

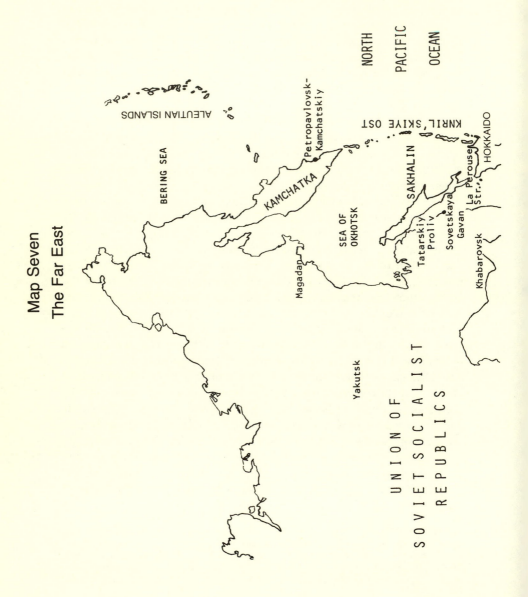

Map Seven
The Far East

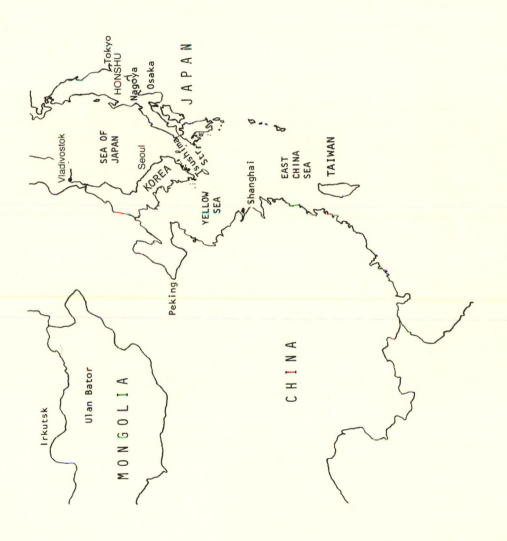

The peacetime and potential wartime projection of military power from the forward positions of the Heartland in Central Europe, in the Kola Peninsula, and in the Far East is a source of major concern to Western defense planners. It would be foolish, however, to ignore the weaknesses of Soviet geopolitics. In time of war, the separate Soviet fleets would have the utmost difficulty reinforcing one another; and interdiction of overland communications and support between the European USSR and the Far Eastern core area would be an elementary matter. Also, the Soviet imperium over Eastern Europe, however useful in military terms, is a permanent source of political anxiety to Soviet officials.

Policy Objectives

Soviet foreign policy may usefully be characterized in terms of a maximum-minimum principle, namely, to seek the maximum gains with minimum risks. Geopolitically, Soviet leaders probably believe that time is on their side; the Soviet Heartland power is permanently a Eurasian power, while the United States, neglecting Mackinder, Spykman, and others, may come to forget that the Eurasian Rimlands are forever the American security dike. For reasons of domestic preoccupation, anger at "ungrateful" allies, or simply psychological distance, Americans might lose interest in balancing power in and around Eurasia. The Soviet Union, by virtue of geopolitical location (not to mention political inclination), cannot lose interest.

Since access to the innermost councils of the Soviet government is not granted, one can only speculate on Soviet policy objectives. It is the contention of this study that there is a logic to East-West geopolitical relations, and a logic to observable Soviet policy actions, which permits the presentation of Soviet foreign policy goals with a fairly high measure of confidence. Soviet deeds, Soviet words, and the more plausible of the geopolitical theories all point in the same direction.

The basic contrast between American and general Western policy goals and the goals of the Soviet Union lies in the stability orientation of the former and the dynamic content of the latter. In the words of one prescient group of American commentators: "Moscow neither believes nor is interested in a world of stable power relations."[56] Over the very long term, Soviet leaders are committed to the concept of victory for their system of ideas/unit of power. The Marxist dialectic, an inherently dynamic framework, has some difficulty coping with the prospect of a world that is in a Communist "steady state." The roles of the Soviet Union as a unit of power in such a world are, to say the least, obscure—even to Soviet theoreticians. The Leninist notion

---

[56] Gouré, Kohler, and Harvey, *op. cit.*, p. 64.

of "the withering away of the state" (the Soviet state!) lacks for official adherents in the Soviet Union. While admitting the existence of these uncertainties well over the horizon, the interim goals of the Soviet Union are very clear indeed. The final confrontation with the United States *may* be very many years away, but Soviet leaders understand very well that they face only one first-class enemy, and that the 1970s is marking a historic shift in the correlation of forces between them.

The Soviet Union appears to set no boundaries to its ambitions—a condition suspiciously reminiscent of Wilhelminian Germany. But unlike Imperial Germany, the Soviet Union is ruled by a committee of cautious bureaucrats who see no necessity for haste or high risk-taking in their policies. In general terms, Soviet policy seems intended to secure improved power relations *vis-à-vis* the United States; and this policy is wholly opportunistic. It is not the case that beyond a current phase of (nonmilitary) struggle, the Soviet Union aspires to a global *modus vivendi* with the United States, on the basis of more advantageous demarcation lines between spheres of influence. In much the same way—and essentially for the same reasons—that there appear to be no *sufficiency* criteria for the Soviet armed forces, so the foreign policy ambitions of the Soviet state are unbounded. At any one time, Soviet policy will show apparent inconsistencies; and local setbacks will be accepted without recourse to military action. What matters is the trend.

Notwithstanding the maximum-minimum principle cited earlier, Soviet leaders are mindful of the possibility that war with the United States could occur. An unplanned crisis could expand either on American (or American-allied) initiative, or the Soviet Union might be confronted with an opportunity for major gains—albeit an opportunity fraught with unusually high risks. While Soviet leaders must hope that perception of Soviet political will and political-military weight, strictly local dynamics, and Western pusillanimity will effect favorable shifts in the balance of superpower influence around Eurasia-Africa, Soviet policy also reveals a profound concern for the course of possible military interactions.[57] Through being the friend that delivers victory, as in Angola, the Soviet Union both encourages the belief that it is the tide of history, and lays the basis for requests for access to territory, sea, and airspace that might be very useful indeed in the contexts of influencing developments in Southern Africa, or menacing the oil supply route from the Gulf to Europe.

---

[57] The basic Soviet strategical-theoretical text remains V.D. Sokolovskiy, *Soviet Military Strategy*, 3rd ed., edited by Harriet F. Scott (New York: Crane, Russak, 1975). Also of great value is the series of Soviet texts currently being published under the auspices of the United States Air Force ("Soviet Military Thought").

Although the European Rimland is the major medium-term prize in Soviet-American conflict, it also happens, by virtue of that fact, to be the area of major risk. Detente, or peaceful coexistence, is an offensive policy; it is intended to help make the world safe for political (and even some military) conflict in areas far removed from the direct military confrontation in Europe. Under the umbrella of detente, the Soviet Union orchestrated military victory for *its* faction in Angola,[58] and earlier had acquiesced in, if not encouraged, the Egyptian-Syrian attack upon Israel on October 6, 1973, and in the Spring of 1975 provided the means for the North Vietnamese invasion of South Vietnam. The essential background to these developments has been the compatibility, in Soviet eyes, of a general policy line of peaceful coexistence in its relations with the West with the purchasing of major new military options relevant to all categories of potential war. The Soviet military build-up needs to be considered in geopolitical perspective.

A. Soviet strategic forces may usefully be thought of as having counterdeterrent, warfighting, and symbolic tasks. If the Soviet Union balances or overbalances the United States in strategic nuclear power, any "extended deterrent" functions of American strategic forces must be subject to severe skepticism. From the late 1940s until the present day, it has always been assumed in the West that American strategic nuclear power was a makeweight compensating for deficiencies in forward-deployed military forces around the periphery of Eurasia (and in and about Europe in particular). Looking to the 1980s, the Soviet Union will have built not merely a balancing counterdeterrent, but also a counterdeterrent that could seize the initiative and hold it.[59] Symbolically, the Soviet modernization and augmentation of its strategic nuclear forces is both an expression of the scale of the Soviet will to power and a source of Western (and other) expectations concerning the confidence with which Soviet theater power might be exercised.

B. Soviet theater forces increasingly have been designed with a view to securing what Paul H. Nitze has termed "projectible power."[60] Because

---

[58] This judgment is not offered in ignorance of the possibility that the Soviet Union may have been at least as concerned to shut out Chinese as American influence in Angola, nor does it deny the high level of active American interest which preceded the overt Soviet-Cuban military involvement. There is some value in John A. Marcum, "Lessons of Angola," *Foreign Affairs*, vol. 54, no. 3 (April 1976), pp. 407-425. This author would draw different lessons from those specified by Marcum, but his indictment of American policy is convincing (whatever one's political orientation).

[59] For justification in detail of these remarks, see Colin S. Gray, *The Future of Land-Based Missile Forces*, (London: International Institute for Strategic Studies, forthcoming).

[60] Paul H. Nitze, "Deterring Our Deterrent," *Foreign Policy*, no. 25 (Winter 1976-77), p. 207.

of the Soviet strategic counterdeterrent, the outcome of military conflict around the periphery of Eurasia-Africa should depend wholly upon the balance of military power deployed in, and deployable to, Eurasia and the marginal seas of Eurasia. The deducible Soviet objective of obtaining as much influence over as much of the Eurasian-African World-Island as countervailing forces will permit requires major investment in both counter-deterrent and "projectible power." This the Soviet Union has been doing and is doing. The Soviet Navy and naval air force, frontal aviation and theater nuclear missile forces, and air mobility—the details in all these areas speak to a determination to be able to match, and overmatch, the traditional superiority of the "projectible power" of the maritime alliance around the Rimlands.

Soviet naval/air reach around the southwestern and southern littorals of Eurasia-Africa is growing and rests upon an expanding set of naval/air facilities (and even bases). To be specific, the Soviet Union is flying maritime reconnaissance missions out of Cuba, Conakry in Guinea in West Africa, Somalia in the Horn of East Africa, and out of Umm Qasr in Iraq. Naval facilities are available on Socotra and in South Yemen (Aden) at the entrance to the Red Sea, a naval base has been constructed at Berbera, and facilities are reported to be used at Mogadishu (Somalia). Also, the Soviet Navy has maintenance and repair facilities at some Indian ports. For southward reach, one must presume that the government of Angola (which is offering almost a classical example of "client" status) would not be in too strong a position to deny base facilities to Soviet ships and aircraft, should such use come to seem expedient. (Mozambique is far less obviously a Soviet client than is Angola; but here again, the Soviet Union does have a potential forward base area; Soviet interest in naval/air facilities in Lourenço Marques has already been expressed.)[61]

It would be easy to exaggerate the significance of Soviet forward deployment in Africa and South Asia. It is sensible to appreciate that the quantity of Soviet naval/air activity in those regions is very limited, and that the "hinterlands" for Soviet bases and shore facilities are politically volatile. But commentators must also recognize that Western naval/air strength in the South Atlantic and the southern Indian Ocean is, as a general rule, distinguished by its absence, that "the Cape route" is literally the energy lifeline of Western Europe, and *the trend* is adverse to Western interests. We may not fear for the 1970s, but what of the late 1980s? Soviet interest in acquiring a large measure of control over Middle East oil supplies, either at source or, if need be, in transit, is sure to be permanent. The

---

[61] Erickson, *Soviet-Warsaw Pact Force Levels*, p. 8.

struggle for the Eurasian Rimlands will not cease. Soviet influence waned in
Egypt, but it remained (though not without strains) in Syria, and waxed
strongly in Libya and Algeria. Soviet presence in the Middle East, South
Asia, and Africa, for reasons fundamentally antipathetic to the NATO
powers, might be expelled by local forces or by NATO action, but it will not
voluntarily be withdrawn. Also over the long term, the Soviet Union will
have to find an enduring solution to its "China problem." The Chinese
threat to the Soviet position in the Far East can only grow, just as China's
alliance value to the West must grow. It is not plausible to maintain that
Soviet leaders will choose to acquiesce in the eventual rise of China to first
class superpower status.

Policy Means and Policy Prospects

To many people in the West, it seems profoundly unsophisticated to
stress either the military dimensions of East-West relations, or military
security questions in international relations more broadly. The real threats
today, so we are told, are to our economic security. The state of the various
East-West military balances is held to be of some residual significance,
though really the military instrument of policy is largely an artifact from
simpler times. This study does not deny that international relations are
highly complex, nor does it challenge the view that there is a very serious
category of economic security issues. Nevertheless, the expansive foreign
policy ambitions of the Soviet Union are no figment of the imagination.
They have been proclaimed with convincing consistency by senior Soviet
officials for many years. Similarly, however old-fashioned it may appear to
some in the West, the Soviet Union acts as though it believes that a truly
major investment in all kinds of military power will bring worthwhile
political-economic dividends.[62]

The history of the Soviet Union reveals one unquestionable success
story, the performance of Soviet arms. Why is the Soviet Union regarded as
a superpower in the 1970s? The Soviet gross national product is probably
less than half that of the United States; the Soviet political system is a source
of acute embarrassment to foreign Communist parties; and its state ideology
is a profound irrelevance both to revolutionary movements and to develop-
ing countries in search of guidance. It might be suggested that the Soviet

---

[62] Detente, in Soviet official explanation for domestic and foreign Socialist audiences, has
been forced on the West as a consequence of the improved power position of the Soviet Union.
The basic Soviet belief appears to be that the better the relative power position of the Soviet
Union, the better are the prospects for "peace" (on Soviet terms). See Gouré, Kohler, and
Harvey, *op. cit.*, particularly ch. 2.

Union is a superpower solely by raw geographical virtue of its power potential—the extent and location of its territory, the number of its people, the quantity and variety of its raw materials, and its advanced state of industrial development. Such a suggestion would be grossly in error; potential counts for little if it is not harnessed. The maritime alliance of NATO could secure a prospectively permanent and major measure of strategic superiority *vis-à-vis* the Soviet Union were it to mobilize its *potential*; but for reasons of political division, domestic-looking choices concerning resource allocation, and a resolute determination not to expect the worst (or even the bad), NATO will be fortunate to avoid a major adverse change in its security condition over the next decade. For all its manifest and profound weaknesses, the Soviet Union has demonstrated that it can compete successfully with the West on one narrow, though critically important, front—the military.

To focus upon the Soviet military instrument is, therefore, entirely appropriate. If the Soviet Union succeeds in establishing its hegemony over Eurasia-Africa, it will be because of the use, the threat of use, or the anticipation by others of the use, of its military power alone. It is sensible to take account of signal Soviet deficiencies—the inefficiency of Soviet industry and agriculture, the ever-present "nationalities" problem, and the rigid and stifling character of Soviet society. But the domestic imperfections of Soviet life will not protect Western countries from defeat, political and military, if the "old-fashioned" threats to military security are not taken sufficiently seriously; many an advanced civilization has gone down before the barbarians. In the words of John Erikson:[63]

> This all comes back to Solzhenitsyn's point that the Soviet leadership may place an undue and obsessive reliance on military force, on its form and function, but then Western Europe has increasingly chosen to ignore the military factor. Between them, these two postures have contributed to what can only be counted a growing imbalance. In the final outcome, Europe may well become that "low-risk option" that will suit the Soviet command perfectly.

Many detailed assessments of Soviet military power are readily available; such exercises will not be reproduced here. But the virtue of a geopolitical perspective is that it does permit a degree of integration and a level of analysis that transcends the familiar partial assessments of the East-

---

[63] "Soviet Military Posture and Policy in Europe," in Pipes, ed., *Soviet Strategy in Europe*, p. 207.

west military balance. The American defense community, for example, has experts on the strategic nuclear balance, theater nuclear, theater conventional, and naval questions; but it has remarkably few people with a competence or even an interest that crosses those necessary but constricting categories of analysis. Unfortunately, competence in analyzing the political meaning of military power is even rarer than competence in more than one of the standard subfields of defense policy analysis.[64] An explicitly geopolitical framework compels both the assessment of *all* categories of military power, and relating that assessment to the political relations of states.

East-West relations in geopolitical perspective pose a terrifying prospect for the maritime alliance. In peninsular Europe, the Soviet Union and its Warsaw Pact dependents have developed a military capability for very rapidly overrunning the American "bridgehead." Opinion is divided as to just how adverse the situation is, but the balance of responsible and knowledgeable analysis suggests that NATO-Europe would lose. As noted above, the Heartland power has succeeded in constructing a strategic nuclear counterdeterrent of such proportions *and quality* that the United States would not be motivated to initiate a major process of nuclear escalation. Unfortunately, the great North American mobilization base for the development and production of the trained manpower and equipment needed to sustain the alliance in a long war in Europe would neither enjoy easy access to the European Rimland, nor would it be likely to find that Rimland in friendly hands when and if its strength did arrive. Soviet naval activity now outflanks the Eurasian-African Rimlands, and threatens to interdict trans-Atlantic (and trans-Pacific) reinforcement and resupply, Also, with base facilities on the Indian and Atlantic Oceans, the Soviet Union would be well placed to interdict the oil supply route from the Gulf.

The threat of Soviet naval and air blockade of the Eurasian-African Rimlands was demonstrated almost arrogantly in the worldwide naval exercise held in 1975—"Okean-75" (or *Vesna-75* in Soviet identification). In this exercise, the Soviet Union employed its ocean surveillance and communication satellites to effect *central* control of naval activity around the globe, while special attention was devoted to the establishment of blockade lines (of submarines) and to counterconvoy tactics. This exercise pointed dramatically to the vulnerability of NATO's western flank.

Much defense analysis suffers from a seeming inability to appreciate that geography imposes different tasks upon the armed forces of the rival alliances. Many Americans appear to have difficulty understanding that if

---

[64] For an analysis of enduring worth, see Klaus Knorr, *On The Uses of Military Power in the Nuclear Age* (Princeton: Princeton University Press, 1966).

they wish to deny hegemony over the Eurasian Rimlands to the Soviet Union, either the maritime alliance must sustain a very robust local denial capability, or the Unites States must invest in a significant margin of strategic nuclear superiority. To recap in question form, How are the Eurasian-African Rimlands to be defended against the Heartland power, if strategic parity (or, more likely, parity-*plus*) is conceded to that power? If superiority *in* the European theater is conceded? And if anyone, worldwide, who can read a newspaper or listen to a radio can learn that the Soviet Union is on the ascendant in gaining influence in potential (and actual) base areas in Africa and South Asia?

If the Soviet Union achieves effective hemispheric denial in the years ahead, the West will have none save its own citizens and leaders to blame. In terms of resources, human and material, the historic bid of the Heartland power for the achievement of hegemony over the World-Island is eminently resistible. Whether or not Soviet leaders and defense planners think in Mackinder's terms, Soviet actions—considered in the round—can be fully comprehended only in a geopolitical framework. The West undoubtedly will awaken to its danger, to the fact that the state of too many military balances has been permitted to erode to its disadvantage; but such an awakening could well occur too late.

4

The United States and the Maritime Alliance: Defending the Rimlands

Her [the United States'] main political objective, both in peace and in war, must therefore be to prevent the unification of the Old World centers of power in a coalition hostile to her own interests.[65]

Insularity: Geopolitical Perspectives

Depending upon the cartographic projection selected, the Americas can be shown to be surrounded by Eurasia-Africa, to surround Eurasia-Africa, or to be an offshore island. Different map projections imply different geostrategic opportunities and vulnerabilities. For example, a global map centered on St. Louis shows the United States either in a favorable central position, able to project power on what appear to be interior air/ocean lines onto the littorals of Eurasia; or, scarcely less plausibly, the central location of the North American land mass on the map suggests that the United States is surrounded by hostile, or potentially hostile, land areas in the east and the west of the Eurasian World-Island. With the completion of the Panama Canal in 1914, the United States became truly an island of continental proportion, capable of projecting power toward the Eurasian Rimlands to the east and west with an ease that could not be matched by Heartland capacity (for several decades).

The compelling logic of geopolitics has indicated to any American capable of reading a map and drawing fairly elementary policy lessons from recent history that Heartland and Rimlands on the World-Island must never be organized by a single political will. Nonetheless, the shape of post-1945

---

[65] Spykman, *The Geography of the Peace*, p. 45.

American policy was dictated far more by events than by geopolitically-educated policy design. The United States anticipated a full-scale military withdrawal from Europe within two years following the surrender of the Third Reich. American forces remained in Europe, first by virtue of occupation rights and duties, and later as a consequence of explicit alliance undertakings, because World War II effected the destruction of the balance of power in Eurasia. For nearly a century (1870-1945), *the* problem in world (that is, Europe-centered) politics had been the difficulty in accommodating a unified and overly powerful and ambitious German state within a European balance of power system. That problem was not resolved until 1945.[66]

Following World War II, it became clear, by 1947-48, that the problem of Germany had been resolved (perhaps temporarily) only at the cost of the elevation of a state which, in its turn, threatened to destroy any aspirations for a functioning balance-of-power system that would be restricted to Eurasia. Despite the enormous damage that it suffered in the "Great Patriotic War," the Soviet Union (apparently, at least) disposed of a "projectible power" potential that could not be countered by strictly Eurasian-Rimland resources. In the late 1940s, China was a great power by courtesy rather than power-produced entitlement; (West) Germany could barely feed itself, let alone function in its time-honored role as a bulwark against the Slavs; while Britain and France, nominal victors in World War II, were reduced to penury. In short, in the period (1946-47) when George Kennan was writing his Mackinderesque recommendation of a firm containment policy, the only question of substance that remained to be debated was over just what kind of containing power really was required.

The pro-Soviet coup in Prague in the Spring of 1948 made clear that the presence of Soviet military power in Central Europe was to be a permanent feature of the political landscape. Without fully appreciating what events had thrust upon it, the United States found itself saddled with the *defensive* Rimland-protective tasks that previously had been borne by the Germans and the Japanese. Leaving aside their more expansive foreign policy ambitions, the Germans and the Japanese had served to check the hegemonial ambitions of the Heartland power. In the 20th century, those peoples had threatened the balance of power in Eurasia by their attempts to conquer the Heartland; but the necessary character of their defensive, checking, roles was inadequately appreciated by many Americans. After 1945, piece by piece, and rarely—if ever—publicly acknowledged in power-political

---

[66] It is possible that this problem is not fully resolved even today. The Warsaw Pact-NATO standoff in Europe has permitted a deferral of the problem of the political future of Germany.

terms, the United States assumed the power-balancing responsibilities of the British Empire,[67] Germany, and Japan.

The events of 1950-51 were most instructive in geopolitical terms. In 1950, the United States assumed the lead in defending South Korea ("a dagger pointing at the heart of Japan"—and also, let it be noted, a natural bridgehead for an eventual contest for control of Northeast Asia); America's China policy, in its strong commitment to the idea of the legitimacy of Chiang Kai-shek's government-in-exile on Taiwan, amounted to a declaration to the effect that the United States considered developments on the Chinese mainland to constitute "unfinished business"; and the United States reversed its policy toward Indochina in favor of the French. These actions in, and policy decisions concerning, the Asian Rimland were linked by a strong thread of internal logic. Specifically, the United States opposed the domination of the Asian Rimland by the Heartland power. It is now customary to deride that logic; with much good reason, it is argued that North Korea, the Chinese People's Republic, and North Vietnam are not compliant clients of the Soviet Union. In other words, the United States foolishly discerned unitary political will where actually there was a diversity of national ambitions.

Over the long run, however, the supposedly naive presumption of the monolithic nature of communism may fare a great deal better than its apparently more sophisticated challengers. If America's capacity for collective action continues to decline, the ability of the CPR to pursue a foreign policy course independent of, let alone in direct and virulent opposition to, Moscow could shrink markedly. As noted earlier in this study, many contemporary strategic-analytical luminaries in the West have virtually no background in history, even very recent history. The geographical location of Indochina renders its harbors and airfields an asset of great importance—particularly for a power totally (otherwise) deficient in forward bases that bear upon the South China Sea and the Southwest Pacific. Vietnam is very much in the Soviet debt. It is not at all implausible to foresee a time when Soviet ships and aircraft will find Vietnamese facilities as useful as did the Japanese. (Skeptics are invited to research the use made of Vietnamese territory and harbors by the Japanese Empire, and to reflect upon the Soviet problems of power projection in the Pacific.)

In 1951, responding to the falsely-identified "diversion" in Korea, the NATO allies effectively began to give their political alliance a quasi-unified military backbone. American leadership of NATO was symbolized by the

---

[67] For an historical perspective on the post-1945 power-balancing role of the United States, see Paul M. Kennedy, *The Rise and Fall of British Naval Mastery* (New York: Scribner, 1976).

appointment of an American general, Dwight D. Eisenhower, to be the first Supreme Allied Commander, Europe (SACEUR). Although "the Soviet threat" (at least as regards any propensity for taking military action) was vastly exaggerated in the early 1950s, and although the United States— under both Democratic and Republican Administrations—did indulge in unduly indiscriminate alliance-creation, the basic idea driving American foreign policy was entirely sound. Without denying that the United States has aided regimes whose only virtue was that they were overtly and noisily anti-Communist, and that the concept of the integrity of the "Rimland Dike" was, for a long period, accepted in an unduly simplistic and total definition, this author would signal a short-list of virtues that permeated what today frequently is called, pejoratively, the "Cold War consensus." The author is not much given to ideological expression, as he has explained elsewhere.[68] He believes that international politics, at root, can be a very rough and nasty business. (Both God-fearing democrats and atheistic totalitarians have been known to drop napalm on innocent or indifferent villagers.) It is appropriate to restate, very succinctly, the core beliefs of that American Cold War consensus that today is held in such widespread disdain. It was (and is still by some) believed that:

1. The United States is the only power which can balance pressure from the Heartland.
2. Some Rimland allies might be politically odious, but it is a certainty that any Socialist-Communist successor regimes would be no better, and would probably be worse. (In the early 1970s, South Vietnam and Cambodia failed to live up to the ideals of Jeffersonian democracy; their American critics have been less than vociferous on the subject of the fundamentally illiberal regimes that now rule those unfortunate countries. This is yet another case of prejudice triumphant.)
3. In the medium term, Western defeat in one locale will weaken resistance elsewhere. The socalled "domino theory," provided it is not interpreted in too mechanistic a fashion, amounts to little more than common sense. The essential accuracy of domino-theory hypotheses was illustrated, sadly, by the easy way in which many of its more strident critics shifted from talking about the war in Vietnam to discussing the war in Indochina in the period 1970-74.

The United States, as a continental-size island bounded on three sides by oceans (the Arctic, Pacific, and Atlantic), could not exist as a function-

---

[68] Colin S. Gray, "Foreign Policy--There Is No Choice," *Foreign Policy*, no. 24 (Fall 1976), pp. 114-126.

ing, unruly democracy were the Rimlands of Eurasia-Africa to be organized into a Soviet security system. Physical survival might be ensured, but the geopolitical isolation of fortress status would promote a fortress discipline and illiberal fortress practices. The principal American political objective in world affairs—today as in 1944, when the words introducing this chapter were written—must be the containment of Soviet (Heartland) power well short of its achievement of hegemony over the Eurasian-African World-Island and the adjacent seas.

The American Style

It was suggested earlier that American political culture was ill-suited to cope with the long-term task of containing the Heartland power. Geopolitical factors require that the American people defend the Rimlands, and relatively free access to the Rimlands, in their own vital interest; yet those same factors inhibit the quality and scale of American performance of that task. Considered in relation to its ease of penetration by Soviet and American power, most of the Eurasian-African Rimlands are, in theory, protected by the fact that oceanic distance and ocean highways *connect* rather than *divide*. In terms of transportation economics, greater distance has little meaning. Save with respect to peninsular Europe (no small exception!), the world's oceans should still be thought of as the interior lines of communication of a maritime alliance that has its heart in a North America that can project power east, west, and north—in many directions—with comparative advantage over the Heartland power of the Soviet Union.

Unfortunately, this neo-Mahanian perspective, analytically respectable though it is,[69] suffers from several critical weaknesses. First, distance is not solely a matter of transportation economics; it has a very strong psychological dimension. In 1938, Neville Chamberlain could dismiss Czechoslovakia as "a faraway country." The British Prime Minister spoke truly for most of his countrymen; in terms of psychological distance, Czechoslovakia was infinitely, mysteriously "Central European"— vaguely romantic, and totally *foreign* and unknown. Few British politicians in 1938 recalled, or more likely had ever known, that Britain's greatest geopolitical theorist, Sir Halford Mackinder, had insisted in his 1919 book that a strong tier of East European states was required if the 700-mile land gateway to the Heartland was to be protected from German ambition.[70] (*"Who rules East Europe commands the Heartland."*) If the defense of

---

[69] See Wohlstetter, *loc. cit.*
[70] Mackinder, *Democratic Ideals and Reality,* pp. 158ff.

Rimland states is, in essence, a matter of comparative advantage in transportation economics, the United States should have secured victory in Vietnam in very short order. The "loss of strength gradient" hypothesis, that power varies inversely with distance, is sheer nonsense in the context of the communications/transport technology of the second half of the 20th century. But human perceptions lend relevance to that (technically) flawed hypothesis. Barring special ties of an ethnic-religious, or even semi-sentimental historical connection variety, it is not misleading to claim that concern, interest, and knowledge do vary roughly inversely with distance. Our minds carry psychological maps, not ton-mile cost-analysis maps. The ability to project power and the will to project power are not at all synonymous—at least with respect to American insular society in the 1970s.

Second, the neo-Mahanian proposition that the maritime alliance has an inherent advantage over the Soviet Union in power projection into the Eurasian-African Rimlands ignores the fact that the Heartland has "gone to sea" in a very serious way over the past two decades. Soviet sea and naval air power could not, at present, deny the United States access to the World-Island, but such a burdensome task need not be contemplated. The Soviet Union has no need to secure "command of the sea" in order to bring the World-Island *effectively* under its control. All that it must accomplish is seriously to hinder trans-Atlantic resupply and reinforcement (or to threaten credibly to do so), or to effect substantial attrition of the supertankers that must navigate half way around the world promontory to meet the absolute energy needs of Western Europe or Japan. The Soviet Navy may, and should, be blown out of the water, its forward facilities on African and South Asian littorals also demolished; but time would not be on the side of the maritime alliance. By compelling the maritime alliance to fight hard for unhindered access to Eurasia, the Soviet Navy would be buying time for Soviet conquest of critical portions of the Rimlands (should Blitzkrieg campaigning overrun its time-table). In the world of the 1980s and 1990s, an eventual *total* naval victory for the United States would be of little value if, meantime, the peninsular European bridgehead were lost.

It is often claimed that physical geography is a neutral factor (or set of factors) in its relation to the inclinations of a society. Oceans will beckon some countries to utilize them as highways for profit and power, and will be seen by other countries as wide moats providing security from contaminating foreign influences. The physical circumstances of the island-continent of North America has helped produce, in its people, a seemingly perpetual dialectic between the urge to withdraw into the illusory safety of a Fortress America, and the impulse to exercise that capacity for transoceanic power projection which a central position between the eastern and western littorals of Eurasia (on some cartographic projections) affords, and which the relative power differential between the United States and the Eurasian Rimlands both permits and requires (if it is not to be engulfed in the security system of the Heartland power).

The insular circumstances of American geography, and the oceanic distances which separate North America from Asia and Europe, continue to have major foreign and defense policy consequences—at the level of perception of enduring interests rather than capability for effective local action. North Vietnamese leaders assessed, correctly, that their stake in the future of South Vietnam was far more substantial than was that of the United States. Americans came, and they would go—the North Vietnamese and their Southern sympathizers would always be there, by virtue of physical and cultural geography. Similarly, Europeans of all nationalities are aware of the geopolitical fact that the Soviet Union is a European power, while the United States is a power in Europe; this is a critical distinction. No NATO-European, however friendly his feelings toward the United States, or trusting his response to contemporary American expressions of enduring alliance fidelity, can afford to ignore the historically well-justified presentiment that the American forward military presence in and about Europe is only a phase in American policy (a long phase, admittedly, but still a phase). NATO-Europeans have to take account of the very probable fact that one day a Mansfield-type amendment will succeed, and that it will precipitate a slide of withdrawal that no President will be capable of arresting (even should he so desire). Transoceanic distance may have lost much of its meaning in terms of the economics of transportation and the speed of electronic communication, but the record of American nuclear strategy belies such economic-geographic common sense.

The geopolitical theories of Mackinder and Spykman, translated for the late 1970s, insist that America's security frontiers are on the Elbe and the 38th parallel in Korea (for prominent examples). Since this is the case, why has the *credibility* of the American nuclear commitment been seen by the United States and allied defense communities as a critical problem? Credibility problems do not pertain to defense of the American homeland, or—in suggestive illustration—seriously to defense of Canada and Mexico. American commitments to the defense of, say, West Germany, are viewed by very many people as being sufficiently "unnatural" in terms of psychological geography that extraordinary effort and ingenuity need to be expended to ensure credible strategic "linkage" between the forward area and the American homeland.

Insular geopolitics do not, in and of themselves, direct societies down one as opposed to other possible paths in internal development or external relations. As noted above, a geopolitical perspective upon international relations requires the commentator to be very attentive indeed to cultural geography. Great Britain, Japan, and the United States have been/are all "island empires" offshore the dual-continent World-Island of Eurasia-Africa, but the differences between them are at least as significant and interesting as the similarities that are traceable to offshore location.

It is possible, though somewhat perilous, to identify the principal characteristics of a distinctive American "style" in foreign affairs. Moreover, as noted with respect to Russia/the Soviet Union, such a style is really the product of domestic experience (though that domestic experience is molded by impinging "foreign" events, just as domestic forces also project outward). This author has long believed that international politics (or relations, for the more inclusive concept), as an aspiring academic discipline, lacked scholarly integrity. International politics are conducted by the human products of distinctive political cultures, and very often in a manner which reflects the rules, practices, and habits learned in domestic political settings. A distinctive American style in the conduct of foreign and defense policy has been manifest, with particular poignancy, in the context of the Strategic Arms Limitation Talks (SALT).

Many Americans today are unwilling to accept that the Soviet Union is committed to a permanency of political struggle with the maritime alliance led by the United States; and is determined to achieve as substantial a measure of strategic *superiority* as it is permitted. The SALT exercise, as a central strand in 1970s-style peaceful coexistence policy, contributes usefully to the psychological disarmament of the West, and encourages manifestations of that apolitical, engineering approach to strategic problems which detracts from American arms competitive performance.[71] The dominant element in the American government seems unwilling, or possibly culturally unable, to take Soviet strategic and arms control (mis)behavior at its face value. Probably because it is a "satisfied" country, deeply wedded to the notion of stability and international order (as a projection of domestic order), and because power accumulation (in readiness for the next crisis and clash of arms) is an idea alien to a society that sees "peace" as the norm, American comprehension of Soviet motives and practices is tenuous at best.

Many American officials and politicians have persuaded themselves that their country and the Soviet Union are committed to a nonviolent search

---

[71] See Colin S. Gray, *The Soviet-American Arms Race* (Lexington, Mass.: Lexington Books, 1976).

for a *modus vivendi* in the world. The SALT enterprise, in this very popular view, is a mechanism intended by *both* sides to constrain the growth (and perhaps the possible character) of rival strategic-nuclear arsenals. Unfortunately, such a world view, with its focus upon stability and order, is very different from everything that we understand concerning the Soviet world view. To Soviet officials, strategic parity is but a passing phase on the road to strategic superiority. In geopolitical perspective, the American defense community has yet to come to terms with the likely consequences of parity, let alone inferiority. Strategic parity means that the United States has no margin of strategic nuclear strength which could be invoked on behalf of endangered friends and allies in Eurasia. One has to presume, on grounds of prudence, that the Soviet Union is devoting (at least) 13 to 15 percent of its GNP to defense for serious political reasons. With an increasingly impressive navy, and with the maintenance of a ground force and tactical air and missile capability that threaten the rapid overrunning of peninsular Europe, the geopolitical implications of the massive Soviet strategic forces build-up become all too clear. That build-up (which even functional apologists for Soviet military power have come to acknowledge as a reality) should secure for the Soviet Union a wide margin of freedom of action against the Eurasian-African Rimlands. Should the United States respond with limited strategic options (LSOs) to calls for help by desperate allies, the Soviet Union could, in the 1980s, reply with a devastating *countermilitary* central riposte that would leave the United States with no sensible strategic options.

A geopolitical perspective upon East-West relations serves to remind Americans that their armed forces have different tasks from those assigned to the armed forces of the Soviet Union. A SALT agreement that plausibly might be defended as a triumph for "the parity principle" should—on very basic geopolitical grounds—be vulnerable to the charge that it licensed roughly equal forces for the support of grossly unequal foreign policy missions. Studies of the Soviet-American or Soviet-NATO naval balance are no less prone to misassessment of the real strength of each side, because the geopolitical asymmetries between the maritime alliance and the Heartland power have not been adequately appreciated. As a consequence of interpretation of its bloody historical experience, the Soviet Union approaches the many questions that bear upon war in what has to be described as a more serious way than does the United States. Both NATO strategy and American strategic nuclear doctrine promise to mesh to the Western disadvantage with what may be inferred, and what is stated by Soviet officials, concerning Soviet approaches to theater conflict and to central war. The United States and its European-Rimland allies are (possibly sensibly) obsessed with the mechanism for providing prewar and intrawar deterrence; a sharp distinction is drawn between deterrence and "war-fighting." In contrast to American practice in Vietnam, the Soviet Union believes that wars should be fought to be won; Soviet "style" was manifest in the interventions in Hungary and Czechoslovakia in 1956 and 1968. Military power on an overwhelming scale was deployed for very rapid results, though for limited purposes.

While the United States, in the best insular strategic style, would be seeking to preserve thresholds and dampen escalation possibilities, the Soviet Union, in the best continental strategic style, would probably be applying massive military force for the end of theater victory. American and Soviet "styles" promise the following character of interaction in conflict. Whereas the United States would be more concerned with limiting military action than securing any outcome definable as victory, the Soviet Union would be more concerned with securing victory than it would with the limitation of military action. The inherent merits in the two distinctive orientations are not at issue here. What is cause for serious concern, if not alarm, is the thought that comparatively few Western officials seem adequately to understand these basic stylistic differences.

In and of themselves, the facts of physical geography in their relation to the political organization of the world are objectively of great importance. But as this chapter in particular has sought to argue, probably of even greater importance are the perceptions of individuals of the political meaning of physical geography, the habits of thought and action that flow from such culturally-bequeathed perceptions, and the policy "lessons" learned (or mislearned) by each society from the assessment and reassessment of its history. The concept of "national style" is clear in outline, yet lends itself to challenge when detail is offered respecting particular nations. Indeed, the difficulty of analyzing style in a rigorous fashion is matched by the importance of attempting such a task.

5

The Lessons of Geopolitics

In terms of resources *that could be mobilized,* the maritime alliance of NATO, perhaps in functional alliance with the CPR, could easily resist outward pressure from the Eurasian Heartland. The geographical gateways into the Rimlands and the open oceans could be utilized as strategic highways in either direction. Foolish inattention on the part of the United States (in particular) to the geographical basis of a balance of power in Europe following World War II did, however, leave the European Rimland with a gross deficiency of territorial depth for the absorption and repulsion of any military thrust by the Soviet Union. Nontheless, the military danger to NATO in Europe, and the political weakness that flows from appreciation of that vulnerability, could be much reduced. Of very recent years, a host of interesting ideas for the better organization of NATO's defenses have been advanced. Some of these ideas even have the rare virtue of being based upon a detailed assessment of probable Soviet "war-fighting" style, likely Soviet objectives, and known—or confidently predictable—Soviet capabilities.[72]

Geopolitics, as presented in this study (it is not denied that there are many partially or totally competing geopolitical worldviews), encourages analysis of the security problems of the West within a global framework—as opposed, for example, to the nonsense of current NATO planning, which has no mandate concerning problems in the South Atlantic or the Indian Ocean. Also, this study finds great merit in the Mackinder-Spykman view that the world, reduced to its power-related essentials, consists of a Heartland superpower that is locked in a permanent struggle with the offshore, insular continental superpower, the United States, for effective control of the Rimlands and marginal seas of the World-Island (the dual

---

[72] See Ken Booth, "Security Makes Strange Bedfellows: NATO's Problems from a Minimalist Perspective," *RUSI Journal*, vol. 120, no. 4 (December 1975), pp. 3-14.

continent of Eurasia-Africa) that sweep in a great arc from Norway's North Cape to South Korea and Japan. The Soviet objective is power—and then more power. Soviet officials take pleasure in the exercise of power, for its own sake; they know that international history is a story of recurrent armed struggle punctuated by armed truce (peacetime, in Western understanding); hence, the more power that is accumulated, the better the Soviet performance should be in the next war. Moreover, Soviet officials appear to understand very well that military power casts a political shadow that may effect Soviet policy goals without need for resort to actual military use.

The strength of geopolitical grand theory is that it places local action, or inaction, within a global framework. The reader may find some of the traditional jargon, or specialized terminology, of geopolitics to be unfamiliar or even mildly distasteful to the point where such usage hinders sympathy for the argument. Political discourse, and even scholarly texts, on security problems in the 1970s tend not to be sprinkled with references to the World-Island, the Eurasian Rimlands, the marginal seas, and the like. The author deliberately has risked such impairment in communication because he wishes to advance the proposition that geopolitical analysis, *qua* geopolitical analysis, is (or should be) a respectable and necessary component in the study of very many defense and foreign policy problems. Just as those who wish to understand nuclear strategy have no choice other than to master the essential concepts of the nuclear strategist (first strike/second strike, counterforce and countervalue, and so forth), so those seeking to comprehend the geopolitical realities of international security questions need to master the essential concepts of the geopolitician.

Evidence that the Soviet Union has transcended its traditional Eurasian land power focus is everywhere to hand. The Soviet Navy now operates in all oceans on a permanent basis. Soviet sea and air power, operating from advanced base areas in the Soviet Union, such as Kola and Kamchatka, from forward facilities in Cuba, East and West Africa, the Arabian Peninsula, Iraq, and India, and on an under-way support basis at sea, now outflanks almost the whole of the Eurasian-African Rimlands. The physical presence, admittedly, is very small in some areas relative to the physical geography, but then so is the physical presence of naval ships and aircraft belonging to the maritime alliance in the South Atlantic, the Indian Ocean, the Arabian Sea, and the Persian Gulf. It is not claimed in this study that the Soviet Union controls or even threatens to control the marginal seas of Eurasia-Africa in any absolute neo-Mahanian sense. What is claimed is that there is a very clear trend in Soviet maritime activity—embracing all categories of sea power (naval, naval air, mercantile marine, fisheries, and

oceanographic research)—which poses a growing threat to Western interests. Port visits by naval vessels and maritime reconnaissance flights may, at
the present time, be largely of political symbolic importance, but they
register, unequivocally, a Soviet commitment to a global role. Also,
skeptics might benefit from the reminder that symbols are important in
politics.

There is nothing that the United States and its allies can do to prevent
Admiral Gorshkov showing the flag wherever his vessels are welcome, or to
discourage World-Island-girdling naval exercises such as Okean-75. But
there is a great deal that can and should be done to arrest and possibly reverse
the adverse trend in the maritime balance in many areas, and to ensure that
the growing challenge at sea does not complement usable margins of
military superiority in Europe and in the strategic nuclear balance. If the
maritime alliance can deny the Soviet Union hegemony over Western
Europe, by whatever means, and if American strategic nuclear power offers
some options that are usable *in extremis,* and are not negated by the Soviet
strategic counterdeterrent, then Soviet gains in the Rimlands outside Europe
are either tolerable or reversible—with the exception of the reforging of a
very solid Sino-Soviet alliance. Lest there be any misunderstanding,
however, it is *not* suggested here that the United States acquiesce in the
defeat of local friends in Africa and Asia.

Any theory, framework, or perspective must simplify in order to
provide focus; the grander and more global the theory, the less the local
detail that will be permitted to intrude. This study has focused upon the
contest between the Heartland of the Soviet Union and the maritime alliance
led by the United States for control, or denial of control, of the Rimlands of
Eurasia-Africa and their adjacent or marginal seas. It is not suggested here
that the Soviet-American power struggle permeates all of international
relations. So long as there is a rough balance of power between the superpowers, local states will tend not to be passive pawns of one side or the other.
In addition, Western interests may be damaged by locally executed policies
that are local in motivation. For example, the partial Arab oil embargo and
fivefold increase in oil prices in 1973-74 was not directly the product of
Soviet policy (although the Soviet Union did arm the states that attacked
Israel, and did—most vehemently—encourage Arab oil producers to
employ "the oil weapon"). On the other hand, the oil embargo did have
meaning in terms of the Soviet-American contest.

Readers should be advised that when this study refers to control or
potential control by the Soviet Union of a particular state or area, the word is
employed more in the meaning of the French *contrôle* (general supervision)

than the English "control" (continuous authority even in matters of detail). A great many of the socalled "debates" that convulse Western defense communities, and which find some usually distorted reflection in the public media, bear witness to the value of the proposition that the geopolitical education of our officials and policy-concerned scholars and commentators is sadly deficient. There should be no need for prudent commentators to have to warn periodically that "the Russians are coming." Soviet intentions are written indelibly in the long course of Russian/Soviet history, in the ideology which Soviet officials are obliged to espouse, and in the general character of international politics. Soviet leaders cannot endorse "the parity principle," a concept of a stable international order acceptable to Americans, or the idea that social-political systems defined as antagonistic to the Soviet Union can have legitimate interests. The Soviet Union, as Russia before it, is an expansionist power that can be contained only by the threat of force and by a manifest, credible (in Soviet eyes) determination to exercise that force. This military orientation reflects the fact that the Soviet challenge essentially is military in character—though for political ends.

National Strategy Information Center, Inc.

STRATEGY PAPERS

Edited by Frank N. Trager and William Henderson
With the assistance of Dorothy E. Nicolosi

The Geopolitics of the Nuclear Era: Heartland, Rimlands, and the Technological Revolution by Colin S. Gray, September 1977

The Sino-Soviet Confrontation: Implications for the Future by Harold C. Hinton, September 1976

Food, Foreign Policy, and Raw Materials Cartels by William Schneider, February 1976

Strategic Weapons: An Introduction by Norman Polmar, October 1975

Soviet Sources of Military Doctrine and Strategy by William F. Scott, July 1975

Detente: Promises and Pitfalls by Gerald L. Steibel, March 1975

Oil, Politics, and Sea Power: The Indian Ocean Vortex by Ian W.A.C. Adie, December 1974

The Soviet Presence in Latin America by James D. Theberge, June 1974

The Horn of Africa by J. Bowyer Bell, Jr., December 1973

Research and Development and the Prospects for International Security by Frederick Seitz and Rodney W. Nichols, December 1973

Raw Material Supply in a Multipolar World by Yuan-li Wu, October 1973

The People's Liberation Army: Communist China's Armed Forces by Angus M. Fraser, August 1973 (Out of print)

Nuclear Weapons and the Atlantic Alliance by Wynfred Joshua, May 1973

How to Think About Arms Control and Disarmament by James E. Dougherty, May 1973

The Military Indoctrination of Soviet Youth by Leon Gouré, January 1973 (Out of print)

The Asian Alliance: Japan and United States Policy by Franz Michael and Gaston J. Sigur, October 1972

Iran, The Arabian Peninsula, and the Indian Ocean by R.M. Burrell and Alvin J. Cottrell, September 1972 (Out of print)

Soviet Naval Power: Challenge for the 1970s by Norman Polmar, April 1972. Revised edition, September 1974

How Can We Negotiate with the Communists? by Gerald L. Steibel, March 1972 (Out of print)

Soviet Political Warfare Techniques, Espionage and Propaganda in the 1970s by Lyman B. Kirkpatrick, Jr., and Howland H. Sargeant, January 1972

The Soviet Presence in the Eastern Mediterranean by Lawrence L. Whetten, September 1971

The Military Unbalance
   Is the U.S. Becoming a Second Class Power? June 1971 (Out of Print)

The Future of South Vietnam by Brigadier F.P. Serong, February 1971 (Out of print)

Strategy and National Interests: Reflections for the Future by Bernard Brodie, January 1971 (Out of print)

The Mekong River: A Challenge in Peaceful Development for Southeast Asia by Eugene R. Black, December 1970 (Out of print)

Problems of Strategy in the Pacific and Indian Oceans by George G. Thomson, October 1970

Soviet Penetration into the Middle East by Wynfred Joshua, July 1970. Revised edition, October 1971 (Out of print)

Australian Security Policies and Problems by Justus M. van der Kroef, May 1970 (Out of print)

Detente: Dilemma or Disaster? by Gerald L. Steibel, July 1969 (Out of print)

The Prudent Case for Safeguard by William R. Kintner, June 1969 (Out of print)

AGENDA PAPERS

Edited by Frank N. Trager and William Henderson
With the assistance of Dorothy E. Nicolosi

Understanding the Soviet Military Threat, How CIA Estimates Went Astray
by William T. Lee, February 1977
Toward a New Defense for NATO, The Case for Tactical Nuclear Weapons,
July 1976
Seven Tracks to Peace in the Middle East by Frank R. Barnett, April 1975
Arms Treaties with Moscow, Unequal Terms Unevenly Applied? by Donald
G. Brennan, April 1975
Toward a US Energy Policy by Klaus Knorr, March 1975
*Can We Avert Economic Warfare in Raw Materials? US Agriculture as a
Blue Chip* by William Schneider, July 1974

OTHER PUBLICATIONS

Arms, Men, and Military Budgets, Issues for Fiscal Year 1978 edited by
Francis P. Hoeber and William Schneider, Jr., May 1977
Oil, Divestiture and National Security edited by Frank N. Trager, December
1976
Alternatives to Detente by Frank R. Barnett, July 1976
Arms, Men, and Military Budgets, Issues for Fiscal Year 1977 edited by
William Schneider, Jr., and Francis P. Hoeber, May 1976
Indian Ocean Naval Limitations, Regional Issues and Global Implications
by Alvin J. Cottrell and Walter F. Hahn, April 1976